COMMUNICATING in the Workplace

The Workplace Skills Series

Dan Farley
Cindy Donaldson

Books Available in The Workplace Skills Series

Communicating in the Workplace

Teambuilding and Problem Solving in the Workplace

To order, call, write, or email:

Work Skills Associates
712 Matadero Ave.
Palo Alto, CA 94306
Phone: (650) 493-8718
Fax: (650) 493-2887
E-mail: wsa@workskills.net
website: www.workskills.net

The Workplace Skills Series

Work Skills Associates
712 Matadero Avenue
Palo Alto, CA 94306
Phone: (650) 493-8718
Fax: (650) 493-2887
E-mail: wsa@workskills.net
website: www.workskills.net

Acknowledgments

Many thanks are in order to people who helped make this book possible.

To Judy Heyboer for starting it all and sponsoring the initial Work Skills Class.

To Ken Coleman at Silicon Graphics for his sponsorship and support. To Caretha Coleman for her support and class visits.

To Pat Mahony, Dave Viale, Neale Mulligan, Helen Schraeder, Brad Bunnin, and Tom Holt for their professional advice and encouragement.

To our valued customers: Mary Hendrickson, Joyce Colvard, Roietta Fulgham, Soledad Santos, Janie Trainor, Sue Hamilton, Terri Morrow, and Randi Barrat-Black. Thank you all for your invaluable advice on the content and your continued support for the curriculum.

To Norma Olmos for sharing her expertise on diversity.

To Jane Hall Taylor for keeping our hands off the keyboard.

To Sylvia Allen for providing the time to make this book possible.

To Trevor Schirmer for getting it all there.

To Manuel Arreola for his great photography work.

To Diana Bonet for her fine editing and advice, and for reuniting those split infinitives.

To Phoebe Bixler for her amazing ability to decipher multiple layers of edits.

To Meredith Williams for being helpful and attentive, but not obsequious.

To Lee Wimberly, wherever you are.

To Tom Farley for his Sunday morning pep talks. To Kay and Dave Farley for their support and interest.

To Robin Weiss for her graphic design expertise, patience, and the friends-and-family discount.

To Stuart for his optimism and encouragement.

And especially to Julie for her patience, invaluable advice, love, and appreciation for the importance of poetry.

Table of Contents

Introduction

If you have had a job, you probably got it after an interview with the supervisor, manager, or perhaps the owner of a business. Most employers interview people before hiring them. No matter how long or tough the session, the interviewer was really trying to answer one major question:

"How can you help me if I hire you?"

Now put yourself in the manager's shoes for a minute. Studies show that managers spend up to eighty percent of their time dealing with "people issues." This includes settling disputes between employees, calming angry customers, and correcting problems caused by poor communication. Eighty percent! Think about that. If your instructor told you that eighty percent of your grade was dependent on whether you were on time, and twenty percent was homework and tests, what would you focus on? Being on time, of course. So if managers spend eighty percent of their day solving communication problems, what do you think they will focus on when they interview you, and ask themselves:

"How can you help me if I hire you?"

The answer is, of course, they will focus on your communication skills. All employers are looking for people who can communicate well, which is why we wrote this book. But there's one more reason why the skills are so important.

Studies show that most people get fired for the following reasons:

- Can't communicate well with others
- Can't work well on a team
- Disorganized
- Late
- Can't follow instructions

People who can't get along well with others usually do not last in a job. Who wants to work with someone they can't get along with? That's the other reason we wrote this book. Communication skills will not only help you get a job; they will also help you keep it.

Communication Skills = $$$!

The communication skills you learn in this book will be valuable both to you and to the organizations you will serve. It would cost an employer up to a thousand dollars to send you to classes to learn these skills, and many companies don't have such resources. By learning these skills now you make yourself a valuable asset to your employers because you will already have the skills; you save the employer money.

Why are we so sure employers are looking for these skills? Because one of the authors, Dan Farley, is a Silicon Valley manager with 15 years of experience managing and training people. The skills you will learn are state-of-the-art communication skills that employers are teaching their employees in a wide variety of work settings today.

You will learn these skills in an interesting, unique manner because the co-author, Cindy Donaldson, is a teacher. In her several years of teaching this class and developing its curriculum, Ms. Donaldson has designed exercises, role plays, and hands-on activities that will help you learn vital workplace skills and remember them long after you have finished the class. Hundreds of students have already taken this course, and many of them have impressed employers and gotten jobs because they understand how to communicate well with people. We encourage you to use these opportunities to practice in the classroom so you, too, are ready for real-life situations outside of class. Finally, we hope you will enjoy learning how to communicate—it is a skill you will use forever!

Knowing Your Style

Each of us is unique because of our individual personalities. If we were all the same, life would be pretty boring. The variety of personalities that we encounter makes every day exciting, although you can probably name examples of situations you find difficult. While some people help you feel comfortable and relaxed, for example, others make you want to run away screaming. This book will help you understand and appreciate different personality styles, so that you have a better sense of how to relate to all kinds of people.

Before you can understand other people, you need to know yourself. Once you understand your own style, you will see how others perceive you, and what is getting in the way of how you see them. You will be able to predict your own reactions to situations, and will be able to give more focused attention to other people.

Your Most Comfortable Style

Would you wear these clothes all year round? Of course not! Personality styles are like clothes; you can adjust them for different situations.

What do you think of when you hear the word "style?" Perhaps you think of clothes. You may have one style that you wear a lot because you like it, but you don't wear that style all the time. Would you wear different clothes if it were snowing and -30° outside, or if the president were visiting the class? Probably. You would adjust your clothing style to one that is right for a situation.

The same is true about the four personality styles that you are about to study. You will probably find one style that fits you best, that you are most comfortable with. But the truth is, given a situation, you can demonstrate any of the personality styles. In this section we focus mostly on the personality style that fits you most of the time, so you can learn more about yourself. Later, you will apply the same styles to learn about other people.

Forcefulness and Outgoingness

In this section, you will study two important characteristics of the four personality styles: how **outgoing** and how **forceful** you are. The degree to which you are forceful or outgoing determines your most comfortable personality style. Here are some examples of the two main behaviors that determine personality styles.

Forcefulness

Highly Forceful People

- Speak loudly and strongly
- Tell people what to do
- Push their opinions or ideas
- Confront conflict
- Like to debate

Less Forceful People

- Speak softly and gently
- Ask people for ideas
- Hold back ideas or opinions
- Avoid conflict
- Don't like to debate

Which person is more forceful? Which one is less forceful? How can you tell?

Outgoingness

Highly Outgoing People

- Show their emotions
- Talk a lot
- Enjoy small talk
- Use gestures while speaking
- Like to work with people

Less Outgoing People

- Hide their emotions
- Use few words
- Avoid small talk
- Stay fairly still while speaking
- Prefer to work alone

Which person is more outgoing? Which one is less outgoing? Why?

EXERCISE: Identifying Your Personality Style

Directions: Below are fifteen rows of words. Each row has four words or phrases on it. For each row circle the two out of the four words that best describe you. It is important to consider each row of four words separately. Words in other rows may seem similar; consider each row on its own. When you are done, count how many circles you have in each of the four columns, and write the numbers at the bottom.

	A	B	C	D
1)	Serious	Aggressive	Carefree	Accommodating
2)	Shy	Impatient	Social	Reasonable
3)	Purposeful	Takes charge	Casual	Follows
4)	Thinking	Headstrong	Feeling	Tactful
5)	Factual	Outspoken	Dramatic	Holds back
6)	Introvert	Controlling	Extrovert	Easygoing
7)	Modest	Firm	Attention-getting	Flexible
8)	Businesslike	Restless	Friendly	Relaxed
9)	Low key	Confrontational	High-energy	Agreeable
10)	Concise	Direct	Chatty	Indirect
11)	Likes it quiet	Daring	Likes parties	Careful
12)	Controlled	Decisive	Animated	Cautious
13)	Unemotional	Forward	Emotional	Reserved
14)	Subdued	Questioning	Dynamic	Accepting
15)	Reserved	Directing	Bubbly	Helpful
SUM				

Directions: Put a point on each axis below to represent your total in that category. Make sure you put one point on the A axis, one on the B axis, C and D. Then, in each quadrant, connect your points by plotting the point where they would meet, forming a square or rectangle:

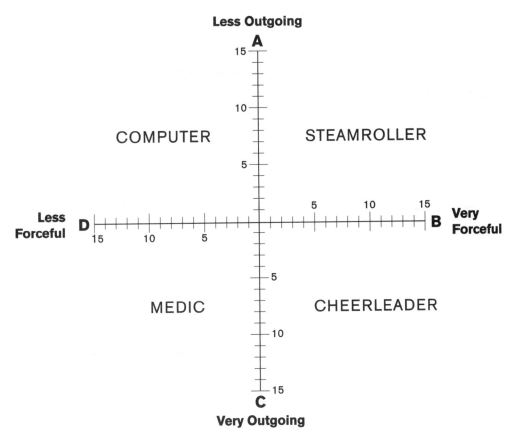

1. In which quadrant is the biggest part of the rectangle? This is your most comfortable style—the style you use most.

Your most comfortable style: _____

2. Now, in which quadrant is the second biggest part of your rectangle? This is your next most comfortable style—your secondary or backup style.

Your next most comfortable style: _____

3. In which quadrant is the rectangle smallest? This is your least comfortable style; you use this style only occasionally, and you use it the least of all four.

Your least comfortable style: _____

As you read the following descriptions, see whether the most comfortable style choice describes you at your most natural. And see if your least comfortable style is totally unlike you.

Cheerleaders

Picture yourself at a football game. The team is on the field, and cheering for the team are the cheerleaders. They are excited about winning the game, and they work to energize the crowd as well. The cheerleaders are noisy and enthusiastic and they love being in front of the crowd. Even if the team is behind, the cheerleaders yell encouragement, helping the team to win.

Cheerleaders are energetic, outgoing people who spread enthusiasm for whatever they are doing.

We use the label **cheerleader** to describe one of the four personality styles, not simply because cheerleaders can do backflips and lead crowds, but because they are energetic. They get excited about things and like others to feel the same way. Because of their enthusiastic nature cheerleaders might seem noisy or pushy. But they are generally well-liked and fun to be around.

Cheerleaders are very outgoing. They are fast paced and they try to include everyone. They don't spend a lot of time thinking about details, which might cause some people to view them as unorganized or careless.

On work teams, cheerleaders are often leaders because of their strong personalities. They tend to talk a lot because they get excited about ideas or goals. They can be impatient if the team gets bogged down in details. Cheerleaders are vital members of teams because they are good at motivating people, are sensitive to the feelings of others, and they have high energy.

Cheerleaders tend to form relationships quickly, and they seek friends who are energetic and like to have fun. Because they are so energetic, they can overwhelm people. Once they form relationships, cheerleaders are resourceful, fun friends.

Cheerleaders look for careers that give them lots of exposure to people and applause. You will find cheerleaders in entertainment, politics, sports, and sales.

Medics

Picture a scene from a disaster movie where lots of people are hurt. Running from person to person is a medic, who is taking care of everyone. The medic is really concerned about everyone, sometimes risking his or her own safety to help. The medic is satisfied only when everyone else has been taken care of.

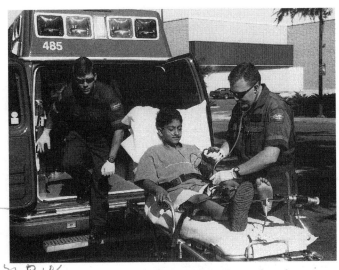

We use the label **medic** to describe one of the four personality styles because they show a lot of concern for the well-being of others. They are eager to please and to help. They are very good at creating friendly relationships with others.

Medics are friendly, relaxed and laid back. They aren't very competitive, and they prefer to let others lead groups. Medics really hate conflict and disagreement because they like to be liked, and they don't want to hurt anyone's feelings. Sometimes they are described as "too nice" or "wishy-washy" because they avoid conflict.

Medics often show a lot of concern for the feelings and well-being of others.

On teams, medics let others lead, but they are very quick to offer help. They do not express their opinions forcefully, and will often wait for others to ask them for feedback. But medics are vital members of teams because they are excellent listeners. Also, because they value relationships, they keep team members working together.

Medics take the time to get to know people. Because they are eager to please and don't like conflict, their own needs or opinions are sometimes overlooked. Once medics create relationships, they are loyal helpful friends.

Medics do well in careers that involve lots of personal interaction and the opportunity to help others. You will find many medics in health care, teaching, child care, counseling, and the ministry.

Computers

The word computer probably makes you think of a machine—usually gray—that processes numbers and prints out information. It makes very little noise, occasionally beeping or humming. Computers are good at processing lots of information, and in today's world we depend on them to manage complex systems like airlines and hospitals.

Computers like facts and data. They are often quiet, and are very good at keeping track of details.

We use the label **computer** to describe one of the four personality styles, not because these people are machines, but like computers, they are comfortable with information, are very good at processing it, and prefer data, numbers, and facts to feelings and emotions.

Computer personalities are quiet and reserved. And they are cautious. Computers hate making a wrong decision, so they gather as much information as possible before stating an opinion or making a decision. Because of this, others sometimes see them as procrastinators.

On teams, computers let others lead, as they prefer to work in the background. They tend to talk less than other personality types, and sometimes need to be drawn out. But computers are vital members of successful teams because they are organized and methodical. They can process mounds of information, and they tend to keep teams grounded in facts.

Computers take time to build relationships because of their caution. They may seem shy, and they can be uncomfortable expressing feelings. But once relationships are established, computers are loyal, steady people who can be counted on.

In working with others, computers might seem perfectionistic and dry. In a group that understands and values its team style, computers are recognized as knowledgeable, organized, and dependable.

Computers look for careers behind the scenes. They are found in such professions as research, engineering, accounting, computer work, science, and mechanical trades.

Steamrollers

Picture a steamroller paving a road. You see a powerful piece of equipment, forging a straight line, flattening everything in its way. In one pass, a steamroller makes a bumpy road smooth. It can do in a few minutes what would take a team of workers many hours.

The label **steamroller** describes one of the four personality styles, not because they flatten others, but because, like steamrollers, they are forceful individuals who are very good at getting things done in a no-nonsense manner, and will move obstacles out of the way if necessary.

Steamrollers are strong willed, direct people. They aren't afraid of conflict, and if they disagree with you, they let you know. Steamrollers like to feel in control, and often take over situations. They don't make much small talk. They get right to the task, and they like things to move along quickly. For these reasons, people might see them as pushy, unfriendly, critical, and rude.

Steamrollers get things done quickly, and will flatten any obstacles in their way.

On teams, steamrollers are often leaders, or at least very vocal members. They like goals, and will push the team hard to reach them. They will become impatient with team members who are too slow, or who are not contributing. But steamrollers are vital members of successful teams because they get things done quickly, and they are very good at clearing obstacles.

Steamrollers take a lot of time to build relationships because they tend to overpower others. They don't always listen, because they are focused on some task or goal. But once they form relationships they are excellent people to have on your side because they are so strong willed.

Steamrollers seek careers that offer opportunity for power and exposure. They like personal success. Steamrollers are often executives, lawyers, military officers, and law enforcers.

Each personality style is a combination of degrees of forcefulness and out-goingness. Each style has some, but not all, characteristics in common with other styles. Understanding the common characteristics among the styles helps you recognize and appreciate differences, and makes you more effective with styles different from your own.

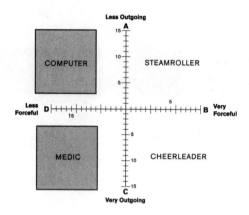

Less forceful styles

Computers and medics share a less forceful nature. Both tend to hold back and let others lead.

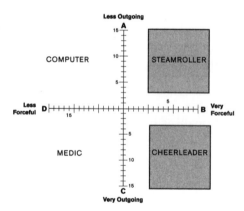

More forceful styles

Steamrollers and cheerleaders share a more forceful nature. Both tend to take control, but in different ways—steamrollers use few words, while cheerleaders are more talkative.

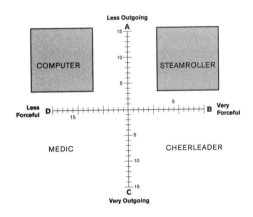

Less outgoing styles

Computers and steamrollers share a less outgoing nature. They don't enjoy lots of small talk, and they use few words to make their points. Steamrollers make their points more forcefully than computers. (Because of their forceful nature, steamrollers are often seen mistakenly as outgoing.)

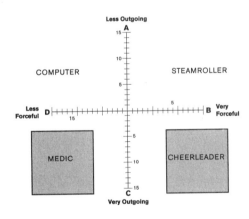

More outgoing styles

Medics and cheerleaders share an outgoing nature. They are talkative and they like social interaction.

EXERCISE: Identifying Others

Directions: Think of different people (friends, family, co-workers, teachers, movie stars, athletes) who fit into these four personality styles. Be ready to share your answers with the class and your reasons why.

People who are cheerleaders

_____

_____

_____

People who are medics

_____

_____

_____

People who are computers

_____

_____

_____

People who are steamrollers

_____

_____

_____

HOMEWORK: Identifying Other Personality Styles

Directions: Now that you've decided on your own personality style, use the information to analyze some acquaintances. Choose three familiar people and describe their personality styles.

Example
Name: Stuart Donaldson
Relationship to you: Husband
Personality style: Computer
Two reasons why you think so: He loves facts and he is never aggressive.

Person #1

Name: _____

Relationship to you: _____ Personality style: _____

Two reasons why you think so: _____

_____

Person #2

Name: _____

Relationship to you: _____ Personality style: _____

Two reasons why you think so: _____

_____

Person #3

Name: _____

Relationship to you: _____ Personality style: _____

Two reasons why you think so: _____

_____

Understanding Other Styles

Now that you've studied the descriptions of different social styles, it may be easier to understand why different people behave the way they do. If your primary style is a computer, for example, you like to operate on a factual level. You may have a co-worker who is always talking about personal stuff, and he makes you uncomfortable. Now you understand that he's not trying to bother you—it's just his style.

The key to successful communication is to remember that everyone is different. Sometimes you have to tailor your own social style to fit someone else's style. Then you put other people at ease, and make them more willing to listen to your ideas.

Because everyone is different, learning how to adjust your style to communicate with others is a very powerful tool!

EXERCISE: What Your Style Prefers

Directions: To begin, reflect for a moment on what puts you at ease in a conversation. Next, think about what things make you feel awkward or annoyed. When you have thought of some, write them below.

Your most comfortable personality style: _____

Three things people do while they're talking to you that make you feel comfortable:

_____

_____

_____

Three things people do in a conversation that make you uncomfortable or mad:

_____

_____

_____

EXERCISE: Other People, Other Styles

Directions: Think of four people in your life who fit each of the social styles. Write each person's name next to his or her social style below. Then, think of something you do when you're talking to each of them that seems to put them at ease.

Example:

Computer	*Bill Gates*	*Likes facts, figures*
Style	**Name**	**What makes them comfortable?**

Cheerleader_____

Medic_____

Computer_____

Steamroller_____

EXERCISE: Hearing From Other Styles

PART ❶

Directions: Please break into teams according to social style. Your team's job is to look at the notes you wrote on the previous page and decide on the top three communication techniques that others could use to make you more comfortable. Then, list the worst three communication mistakes people could make around you.

Your team's social style:_____

Top three techniques:

_____

_____

_____

Worst three mistakes:

_____

_____

_____

PART 2

Directions: Finally, select one person from your group to share your results with the rest of the class. Copy the responses of the other social styles so that you have information to use in the future when you must communicate with different styles.

CHEERLEADERS

Three good techniques   Three mistakes to avoid

1. _____   1. _____

2. _____   2. _____

3. _____   3. _____

MEDICS

Three good techniques   Three mistakes to avoid

1. _____   1. _____

2. _____   2. _____

3. _____   3. _____

COMPUTERS

Three good techniques   Three mistakes to avoid

1. _____   1. _____

2. _____   2. _____

3. _____   3. _____

STEAMROLLERS

Three good techniques   Three mistakes to avoid

1. _____   1. _____

2. _____   2. _____

3. _____   3. _____

HOMEWORK: How to Adapt to Other People

Directions: Read the following situations. Think about the person each one describes. Decide which personality style each person is, and which techniques you might choose in order to communicate well.

1 Lisa is a co-worker in your department. She is fun to work with and she is always upbeat and optimistic. People often stop by to talk with Lisa in her office, because she usually has a joke or a funny story.

You run a weekly meeting that Lisa attends. While Lisa actively contributes, she also tells lots of jokes and distracts others. Her behavior is starting to hurt the productivity of the meeting. You need to approach her about this.

Lisa's personality style is _____

When you talk to her, remember to

_____

_____

Make sure that you don't

_____

_____

2 Your neighbor, Alan, is a nice guy, but fairly quiet. He often works on his fishing equipment in his very organized garage. Alan is friendly, but pretty factual. When he talks about his fishing trips he gives you specific details, like exactly where he fished, what equipment he used, the size of the fish, etc.

Alan keeps his fishing boat in his driveway, and it blocks the sidewalk. Several times your kids have run into it. You need to approach Alan about this.

Alan's personality style is _____

When you talk to him, remember to

_____

_____

Make sure that you don't

_____

3   Your boss, Terry, is very demanding, both of herself and of others. When speaking, she gets to the point quickly. When she gives directions, she expects them to be followed, and completed on time. Last Wednesday Terry asked you to organize all the files for the office by two o'clock today.

You organized the files, but you have lost the key to the cabinets! Since all the cabinets are locked, you will not be able to show Terry your work at two o'clock. How will you tell Terry about the situation?

Terry's personality style is _____

When you talk to her, remember to

_____

_____

Make sure that you don't

_____

_____

4   You ride in a carpool with Mike, who is a very friendly guy. He likes hearing about how your job is going as you drive to and from work. When problems come up at your work, he is good at listening to the situations you describe and understanding the issues you are facing.

There is one big problem, though: Mike drives way too fast. You must talk to him about slowing down, because you are often frightened when he is driving.

Mike's personality style is _____

When you talk to him, remember to

_____

_____

Make sure you don't

_____

_____

5   You share an apartment with Julie, who is generally a great person to be around. She has lots of friends and enjoys giving parties and having people over. She can always think of something interesting to do when the two of you get bored.

Recently your brother called and said he needs to sleep on your couch for two weeks while he finds a new place to live. You have to approach Julie to get her okay for this.

Julie's personality style is _____

When you talk to her, remember to

_____

_____

Make sure you don't

_____

_____

6   Your co-worker is Ted. He is very organized. When you go to meetings, Ted is pretty quiet, but when he speaks he always knows his facts. Ted understands his job very well, and you often ask him questions because you know he will give you correct information.

Your boss just gave you a new assignment. In order to do it right, you could really use Ted's help, but it will take quite a bit of his time. You want to approach him and ask him for his help.

Ted's personality style is _____

When you talk to him, remember to

_____

_____

Make sure you don't

_____

_____

HOMEWORK: Who Said That?

Directions: In the list of statements below choose which personality style is the most likely to have made that comment. Fill in the appropriate letters as follows:

Cheerleader = Ch; Steamroller = S; Medic = M; Computer = Co

1. _Ch_ "It is so exciting to be here!"

2. _M_ "How have you been doing?"

3. _Ch_ "Come on! This will be fun!"

4. _Co_ "What's the bottom line here?"

5. _Co_ Prices have risen 15.25 percent in the last three-and-a-half months."

6. _S_ "There are a few details you might be overlooking here."

7. ___ "How was your weekend? Did you enjoy your time off?"

8. _Ch_ "I'm bored. We're getting bogged down in the details."

9. _S_ "Have you considered all the costs of the advertising campaign?"

10. _M_ "All right, this is what I think we should do."

11. _S_ "We don't have all day to hear everyone's ideas."

12. _S_ "I'd like to make sure we hear from everyone before we move on."

13. _Co_ "How much time will each of the steps in your proposal take?"

14. _M_ "Whatever the group wants to do is fine with me."

15. _M_ "What do we need to do to get this sale?"

Name:_____

HOMEWORK: Who Did That?

Directions: Below is a list of actions that certain styles might take. Consider each one and choose which personality style is the most likely to take this action.

Fill in the appropriate letters as follows:

Cheerleaders = Ch; Steamrollers = S; Medics = M; Computers = Co

1. _S_ In a meeting room, they would stand up and change the thermostat if they were cold.

2. _Co_ After a two week vacation, they would spend most of Monday morning telling people the details of their trip.

3. _Co_ This style reads the computer manual before putting the system together.

4. _S_ They are tough negotiators when buying a car.

5. _M_ They would ask everyone in a meeting if they feel cold before they change the thermostat.

6. _Ch_ They don't pay attention to the details regarding extra charges when buying a cell phone.

7. _M_ They would have one or two in-depth conversations at a party.

8. _Ch_ They would collect a lot of business cards from other people at a sales conference.

9. _S_ They would confront someone who cut in line at an airline ticket counter.

10. _M_ They would recognize the quiet contributions of several members of a project team.

11. _M_ They make a point of hearing someone who keeps getting interrupted by others at a meeting.

12. _Co_ They prefer to send an e-mail rather than make a presentation.

13. _M_ They are served the wrong order in a restaurant, but eat the meal anyway.

14. _M_ They are frequently asked, "What are your thoughts?" at the end of a meeting.

15. _S_ They frequently try to order something that is not on the menu.

Being Effective with Other Styles

Stretching

To communicate effectively, you must build trust. We tend to trust what we already know or are used to, whether that be food, clothes, a language, or how someone approaches us. To build trust with others, especially people of different personality styles, try a technique called **stretching**.

Think of a rubber band that stretches into lots of different lengths and shapes. No matter how far you stretch, it is still a rubber band; it doesn't become steel or plastic. And when you let go, it returns to its original shape.

Similarly, building trust with other personality styles means stretching your style a bit, but still maintaining who you are. It means using behaviors that will make someone comfortable with your approach, and more likely to want to communicate with you. If someone is not comfortable, he will resist you, maybe even attack you verbally and make further communication difficult.

Tanisha Stretches to Andrew's Style

Here is an example of how different personality styles can stretch to accommodate each other. Tanisha's most comfortable style is a steamroller. She gets right to the point when she needs something. Her co-worker, Andrew, is a medic. When he sees somebody, he wants to spend a minute chatting to catch up on things; then he can talk about his needs. Tanisha needs a ride to work. Which approach do you think will work best with Andrew?

#1: Tanisha: "Andrew, my car is broken. I need a ride to work. You live near me, so you can give me a ride. Pick me up at 7:45."

#2: Tanisha: "Hi Andrew! How's your job going? Good! Hasn't it been busy the last few weeks? Listen, my car isn't working and I'm having trouble figuring out how I'm going to get to work. Is there a way you could give me a ride?"

If you picked #2, you're right! What might have happened if Tanisha had used the first approach? Her direct, bossy manner would have upset a medic like Andrew, and he might have made up an excuse. In addition, he would have felt resentful and distrustful of Tanisha. By contrast, when Tanisha asked how Andrew was doing, she made him feel comfortable. Then she asked for his help—Andrew's specialty as a medic.

Notice that in both examples, Tanisha was asking for a ride to work. She didn't give up on what she needed. She just asked for it in a manner that Andrew could accept. That is **stretching**.

Building Trust Quickly

Most times you don't know a person's personality style right away. You can't ask strangers or customers to do a personality exercise before you talk to them! So you must be able to identify basic communication tendencies quickly so you can stretch to match their style.

Here are two quick and easy ways to figure out how people communicate:

1. Watch how they move.

2. Listen to what they say.

Observing these two indicators and stretching subtly to match someone's style are very powerful communication tools. Both are explained on the next few pages.

Watch How People Move

Body Language

Body language communicates so much about us. What message do you get from this person's body language?

When you talk you use far more than words to send your message. Your posture, facial expression, and gestures all influence greatly the way you come across. These subtle ways of using your body send a message so powerful they are referred to as **body language**.

In fact, studies show that when you talk your words account for only 30 percent of your message. Your listeners base the remaining 70 percent of their evaluation on what you do with your face, gestures, and tone of voice as you talk. So it is extremely important to be aware of what your **body language** is saying. For example, if a friend tells you she's happy to see you, but then she looks away, slouches, and sighs, do you believe her?

You can use **body language** to improve your ability to communicate. Most people respond more readily to communication styles that are similar to their own. For instance, a cheerleader responds more easily to someone who is enthusiastic and animated than to someone who remains reserved and still. So one way to stretch to meet someone's communication style is to match subtly the way they use body language.

What message do you get from the body language of this person?

Be Subtle!

Subtle is the key word here. If people think you are imitating them they will be suspicious or insulted. But if you use body language similar to theirs, you are stretching your style. Most people become more receptive, often without realizing it! Subtle stretching is a very powerful communication tool.

What To Watch For

When you first meet people, notice how they handle themselves. Watch their body movements. Your goal is to stretch by matching their behavior subtly. Here are some things to look for:

animated

- Do they show lots of enthusiasm, or are they calm?

- Do they lean toward you, or away from you?

- Do they talk quickly or slowly?

- Do they seem pressed for time, or relaxed?

- Do they look you in the eye, or do they avoid eye contact?

- Do they talk about their personal lives, or are they strictly business?

- How is their posture? Slouched? Straight? Legs crossed?

How would you match subtly the body language of this person?

Add some of your own:

- _____Smile_____

- _____

- _____

Once you have noticed some of these behaviors, start to match them. Don't be obvious! Subtlety is the key. If you copy every move, he will think you are strange or insulting. Aim to help him feel at ease by using a similar body language style.

... of this person?

Listen to What They Say

Words, and the way people say them, are other indicators of a preferred communication style. As you recall, two characteristics that determine personality style are forcefulness and how outgoing someone is. Here is a review of each.

Forceful People

- Have strong voices; talk fast
- Approach quickly
- Are not afraid to disagree
- Tell people what to do
- Look at you frequently

Less Forceful People

- Have soft voices; talk slowly
- Approach more slowly
- May hold back true opinions
- Ask people what to do
- Look away more often

Outgoing People

- Move when they speak
- Love to work with others
- Are chatty; like small talk
- Talk about their feelings
- Are playful

Less Outgoing People

- Stay still when they speak
- Prefer to work alone
- Are quiet; avoid small talk
- Talk about facts
- Are serious

The second step in **stretching** is to **listen to how people talk**. Decide their level of forcefulness and outgoingness, and match it subtly, just as you did with body language.

For example, a woman who walks up to you and says confidently, "You. I need your help. Now!" might be a steamroller, but you don't know. You do know she spoke forcefully, so responding with brief, strong words is a way to stretch to her style.

Remember, the way you stretch with your words, body and voice depends on the way other people use theirs. Everyone is different, so watch and listen before you stretch!

EXERCISE: More Practice Building Trust

Directions: Pair up with a partner. There are two roles in each problem set: one is above the dotted line, the other below. Take turns acting out these parts, but remember: Partner #1 does not read anything below the dotted line. Partner #1 will start each conversation.

PROBLEM ❶

Partner #1

You own the Zippy Delivery Company. Your drivers pick up and deliver urgent orders for customers. You need to raise prices because auto insurance costs have risen dramatically and recently you have given raises to some of your most reliable drivers. One of your best customers is Parts World, a big auto parts distributor. Your drivers deliver parts to many auto shops for Parts World. You have to tell the owner of Parts World, Chris, about the price increase, but you don't want to upset Chris and lose the account.

- -

Partner #2

You are Chris, owner of the Parts World auto parts company, and you use Zippy Delivery Service to deliver parts quickly to mechanics all over the local area. They provide good service and save you the expense of buying delivery trucks and hiring drivers. The owner of Zippy Delivery Service is going to tell you he has to raise prices.

Your style: Steamroller

- Very forceful
- Not outgoing

You'll agree to the price hike if he or she:

- Gets to the point right away.
- Explains quickly why prices are going up.
- Gives you all the facts and figures.
- Is open to offering other services (faster delivery, longer hours) if you accept.

You'll find another delivery service if he or she:

- Doesn't get to the point.
- Doesn't explain quickly the reasons why.
- Seems afraid of you.
- Is unwilling to negotiate a few "extras."

PROBLEM ❷

Partner #1

You are an employee at a retail store (The Gap, Tower Records, etc.). You have been working there for six months, and you believe that you have been a valuable employee.

You think that it's time for you to get a raise. You know that a co-worker has also been asking for a raise, and that only one of you will get it. Talk to your boss and ask for a ten percent raise.

Partner #2

You are a manager at a retail store (The Gap, Tower Records, etc.). You have the power to give or deny raises. The person across from you is a pretty good employee, and wants a raise.

The problem is that you have only enough money to give one raise, and another employee is asking for it as well. Conflict makes you very uncomfortable, so you change the subject whenever anyone tries to talk about raises.

Your style: Medic

- Low forcefulness
- Very outgoing

You'll give your employee the raise if he or she:

- Goes with the flow for a while when you change the subject
- Brings up the topic of the raise gently
- Sympathizes with your decision and knows you're in a hard position
- Is nice, positive, understanding
- Can see both sides of the decision
- Smiles a lot

You'll totally drop the subject of the raise
and refuse to talk about it if your employee:

- Gets pushy or aggressive
- Is frustrated and tense
- Refuses to discuss anything about the raise
- Is negative about anything
- Makes you feel bad

PROBLEM ③

Partner #1

You just got pulled over by a police officer for driving 35 in a 25 mph zone. Your exercise partner is the police officer. You're going to try to get out of your ticket because you saw a sign just a block back that said 35 mph, so the speed limit changed suddenly and was not well marked. Go for it!

Partner #2

You are a police officer. You just pulled over your exercise partner for driving 35 in a 25 mph zone. You know it's a speed trap, because the sign that shows the speed change from 35 to 25 is somewhat hidden behind a tree. But it's almost the end of the month, and you haven't filled your quota. And you have a headache.

Your style: Computer

- Low forcefulness
- Not outgoing

You'll let the driver off with a warning if he or she:

- Is calm
- Is polite
- Admits to going 35, but gives a logical argument
- Doesn't interrupt you when you talk
- Doesn't get emotional—angry, upset, teary, etc.

You'll give the ticket to the driver if he or she:

- Becomes pushy or aggressive
- Gets loud
- Lies about how fast he or she was driving
- Won't listen to reason or says that you are wrong
- Is sarcastic

PROBLEM ④

Partner #1

You have a neighbor who works for a company that you've been trying to join for a long time. You just heard about an opening as a computer technician at the company, and you think you'd be an excellent candidate for the job.

Since the company has such a great reputation you want your neighbor to hand in your resume and give the hiring manager a good word about you. Good luck!

Partner #2

You work for a great company, and frequently people ask you to help them find jobs at the company, which your neighbor is about to do. As a cheerleader, you only do that for people who are truly excited about working there and excited about their careers.

Your style: Cheerleader

- Very outgoing
- Very forceful

You'll put in a good word if your neighbor:

- Approaches you in a friendly, upbeat manner
- Is enthusiastic about working at the company
- Would enjoy a career as a computer technician
- Smiles and gestures

You won't put in a good word if your neighbor:

- Is too serious or reserved
- Isn't enthusiastic about working at the company
- Just wants a job
- Doesn't show excitement about being a technician

PROBLEM ❺

Partner #1

You share a house with someone. Your housemate drives a car that leaks a lot of oil on the driveway. The mess is causing problems; the oil is tracked into the house and is staining the carpet. You've gotten it on the floormats of your car, which you like to keep very clean. You want your housemate to fix the car.

Partner #2

Your car leaks a lot of oil on the driveway at home. You don't know much about cars, and hate going to a mechanic because you are afraid you'll be over-charged. It's much easier to put in oil than to fix the leak, even though you know it's making a mess. Your housemate is going to ask you to fix the problem.

Your style: Medic

- Low forcefulness
- Very outgoing

You'll get the problem fixed if your housemate:

- Brings up the topic gently
- Explains why the oil is causing a problem
- Understands that it's hard to get it fixed
- Gently asks if you can have the car repaired

You won't get it fixed if your housemate:

- Gets pushy or aggressive
- Tells you to fix it right now
- Blames you for the problem
- Is negative about anything
- Makes you feel bad

PROBLEM ⑥

Partner #1

You need a favor from a co-worker. The two of you are part of a team working on a project. You volunteered to write a report, but didn't realize you also had to create lots of graphics, which you don't know how to do. Your co-worker does, but will have to stay late to help you meet the deadline. Try to convince him or her to help you out!

Partner #2

Your co-worker is asking for a favor. He or she needs help with some tricky computer graphics for your team's project. The only way you can help is to stay late, which means you'll eat late, go to bed late, and be grouchy tomorrow.

Your style: Steamroller

- Very forceful
- Not outgoing

You'll help your co-worker if he or she:

- Gets to the point–tells you why he or she needs your help
- Admits the mistake
- Is calm and rational
- Looks you in the eye and speaks confidently

You won't help if:

- He or she is too wordy
- Doesn't tell you what he or she needs
- Makes the problem sound like your fault
- Gets emotional
- Seems afraid of you
- Starts to whine or beg

HOMEWORK: Building Trust – "Oops!"

Directions: Describe what might happen if you made the following mistakes.

Example:
*You **are not** forceful with a steamroller.*

If you are not direct, the steamroller might ignore you or get frustrated with your passive style, and demand, "Get to the point! What do you want?"

1. You act forcefully with a medic.

2. You are wordy and expressive with a steamroller.

3. You are very outgoing with a computer.

4. You are extremely reserved with a cheerleader.

Starting Difficult Conversations

There are two ways people can upset you: they can **say** things or they can **do** things that bother you.

Annoying things people say:	Annoying things people do:
• Call you names	• Laugh at you
• Put down your ideas	• Show up late
• Lie to you	• Break agreements

Avoiding an upsetting situation is like hiding in the corner. It doesn't solve anything!

Avoid or Explode

When someone upsets us we typically react in one of two ways: **avoid** or **explode**.

When we **avoid** an upsetting situation we are avoiding conflict. No one likes conflict, so it seems easiest to ignore it and hope the problem goes away. Sometimes people will stop the annoying behavior, but many times they won't.

When we **explode** in a tense situation we yell, scream and sometimes even hit the person upsetting us. While it may feel good to lash out, exploding almost always damages the relationship, and it usually solves nothing.

Sometimes we do both: avoid and explode. At first we ignore the upsetting behavior until we can't take it anymore, then we explode. Neither extreme works, whether alone or in combination.

An effective behavior that avoids the two extremes is called **"Starting Difficult Conversations."** It is a way to confront someone to get your needs met (doesn't avoid), while showing respect for the other person (doesn't explode).

Exploding often makes things worse. It doesn't solve anything either!

The Five Steps to Starting Difficult Conversations

There are five steps involved in starting difficult conversations. Learn them well because you will find that the ability to apply them is a communication tool you will use for the rest of your life. The five steps are:

1. **Check the timing.**

2. **State the facts.**

3. **State your feelings.**

4. **State your needs.**

5. **Ask the other person to respond.**

These steps are described on the following pages.

Check the Timing

If you really need to talk with people, they must be ready to listen. People will not listen if they are tired, busy, or upset. Therefore, the first step in starting a difficult conversation is to **ask about timing**. Here are some examples:

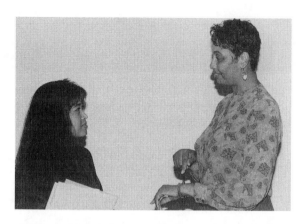

Asking someone, "Do you have a minute?" is a good way to check your timing.

Correct:

"Mike, do you have a minute to talk about something important to me?"

"Jennifer, may I talk to you about a sensitive issue?"

"Boss, can we talk privately?"

Incorrect:

"Sit down and listen to me."

"We've got to talk, now!"

"All right, here's how it's going to be."

If he says he can't talk now—either because he is busy or because he wants to avoid the issue—say something like:

"Can you tell me when a good time would be?"

"When can I come back to talk with you?"

EXERCISE: Other Timing Questions

Directions: Think of three more ways to check the timing with someone.

Example:
"Can we talk privately?"

1. _____

2. _____

3. _____

State the Facts about the Situation

When you have a need to start a difficult conversation it is usually because something has upset you. In the next step, **stating the facts**, you must describe the specific behavior that concerns you. In this step use facts, not your opinions.

Use Facts, Not Opinions

When we try to talk to someone about a sensitive matter we will always get into trouble if we state personal interpretations or opinions rather than facts. When you state a cold, hard fact that you can *prove*, no one can stay angry at you because you are telling the truth. But if you start with your personal interpretation of the facts, that person is likely to feel accused, insulted, and furious. So stick to undeniable truths.

Fact: "You borrowed my computer without asking."

Opinion: "You're rude!"

Fact: "You were late three times this week."

Opinion: "You don't care about me!"

Fact: "I noticed you checking my timecard."

Opinion: "You don't trust me!"

Which is a fact and which is an opinion?

"You jammed the copier and left without fixing it."

or

"You're irresponsible!"

Act Like a Reporter

One way to use facts and not opinions is to think of yourself as a reporter describing a scene. A good reporter always relates facts, not opinions. Let's say a carpool partner often picks you up late. A reporter would describe the situation like this:

Fact: "Twice this week Bob was late picking up Jim for work."

not

Opinion: "Bob is a disorganized slob who doesn't care about
Jim at all and twice picked him up late."

Now, suppose you were Jim confronting Bob. The facts would be something like this:

"Bob, may I talk to you for a minute? Twice this week you've picked me up late for work ..."

Imagining yourself as a reporter helps you stick to the facts, and keeps you neutral, detached, and effective at pointing out problems.

Be like a news reporter. State the facts of the situation, not your opinions.

Starting Words

Starting words are very important in stating the facts. Starting words are the first words you choose to describe the facts. When you begin your statements, try words like:

"I noticed … "

"Three times this month you … "

"You just … "

"At the meeting you … "

"When you … "

Examples:

"I noticed you've been using my computer lately."

"Three times this week you were late."

"You just called me a loser."

"Always" and "Never" Cause Trouble

Avoid absolute words like "never" and "always" because the other person will find examples to counter your statement, and your discussion will go nowhere.

Examples:

> Santos: "You are always borrowing money from me!"
>
> Kim: "That's not true! Last week I borrowed it from John!"

or

> John: "You never clean the bathroom!"
>
> Rick: "Yes I do! I cleaned it three weeks ago!"

Using these words will get you into trouble.

EXERCISE: Other Starting Words

Directions: Below are some possible starting words to describe facts. Fill in some of your own:

1. "You just …"

2. "Three times this week/month/etc.…"

3. "When you …"

4. _____

5. _____

6. _____

EXERCISE: Stating Facts or Opinions?

Directions: Pair up with a classmate. Take turns looking around the room or at each other and then make facts statements to each other. Give each other feedback on whether a statement is fact or opinion. Also note the use of "always" and "never." Do three each.

For fun, try throwing in an opinion or an "always" or "never" statement to see if your partner catches it. Here are some examples:

1. "You are wearing a red sweater." (fact)

2. "Jack wears strange clothes." (opinion)

3. "You always borrow paper from me." (always!)

HOMEWORK: Facts or Opinions?

Directions: Read each of the following statements. If a statement is a fact, put an F in the space beside it. If it is an opinion put an O.

____ **1.** I noticed that you were late for the ten o'clock meeting.

____ **2.** You are irresponsible.

____ **3.** You didn't return the truck keys.

____ **4.** You were late for the ten o'clock meeting on purpose.

____ **5.** You forgot to give me the report.

____ **6.** What you did was stupid.

____ **7.** Your ideas are strange.

____ **8.** You interrupted me three times in the meeting.

____ **9.** You always call in sick on Mondays.

____ **10.** You're trying to make me look bad.

____ **11.** I'm underpaid.

____ **12.** You took ninety minutes for lunch.

____ **13.** You never listen to me.

____ **14.** Several of your e-mails were ten pages long.

____ **15.** I'm paid less than the rest of my co-workers.

State Your Feelings

Once you have described someone's behavior as a fact, the next step in starting a difficult conversation is to **describe your feelings** about it. This gives the other person some insight into the effect that the behavior has on you.

Not Just Touchy Feely

Some people shy away from stating their feelings because it seems "soft" or "touchy-feely." Like anything that is overused, expressing your feelings too often or in too much detail is ineffective. However, stating your feelings is also a powerful tool, and a very effective way of getting what you want, especially when people do not want to cooperate with you. Here are some reasons why.

People Do Not Realize

Have you ever done something unconsciously such as kicking the seat in front of you in a movie theater or tapping your pencil on a table when someone, seemingly out of nowhere, barks, "Will you stop that!" You were probably surprised by such a strong reaction, because you had no idea you were irritating them.

We all do things unintentionally that irritate others. Conversely, others unintentionally do things that bother us. Further complicating the issue is the fact that we all have different ways we want to be treated. What works for you may not work for others. You may not care if people interrupt you at meetings because you like fast-paced give and take. Other co-workers may find interruptions offensive.

We all have certain ways we want to be treated, but we all don't have the same standards. One reason this step—stating your feelings—is important is that people don't know how we want to be treated. So we have to tell them.

Only You Own Your Feelings

Imagine that you are riding in a car with Fred and the air conditioning is on. You say, "Would you mind turning down the air conditioning? I feel cold."

Now imagine that Fred responds, "You're not cold." Doesn't that sound strange? It is, because no one knows how you feel but you. When you say, "I feel frustrated," or "I feel angry," no one can say, "No you don't," because you are speaking for yourself as only you can.

In Most Workplaces, You Have Recourse

Most companies work hard to create pleasant environments where people feel comfortable working. All employers know that hostile work environments and harassment can be very costly issues. When employees speak up about behaviors that make them feel uncomfortable or threatened, most employers will take quick action.

Suppose you have a co-worker who is rude. He often makes insulting remarks to you. You ask him to stop, but he keeps on. After trying unsuccessfully to handle the situation yourself, you bring it to your supervisor's attention. In today's workplace most supervisors know that they are legally obligated to address issues that might create a hostile environment for an employee.

In the workplace, if you say to someone, "I feel uncomfortable when you do that," they have an obligation to change the behavior, or else you can seek action from higher management. (This assumes that your request is reasonable. Requests for someone to stop calling you names or to stop commenting about your appearance are examples of reasonable requests.)

Most—but not all—employers will take such situations seriously and address the behavior quickly. Therefore, saying, "I feel uncomfortable when you do that," is not weak or soft; in fact, it is very strong language because in most workplaces you have recourse if people do not change the behavior that is causing you discomfort.

Feeling Words are about You

When someone has done something to upset you, most of your focus is on that other person. You are intensely aware of their upsetting behavior, and you have a clear picture of what you want them to do differently. But this step, stating your feelings, forces you to focus on yourself. It is very important to be able to describe your feelings in response to another's behavior, so the other person can understand the effect it is having. Without this step, they may not understand why they should change the behavior. Describing your feelings clearly and succinctly helps them understand. It usually takes no more than two or three words. Here are some examples:

"I feel upset."

"I feel frustrated."

"I feel angry."

"I feel uncomfortable."

To express your feelings, you do not always have to use the word, "feel." There are other ways. Here are some examples:

"I'm frustrated."

"I am upset."

"This is irritating to me."

We have broken down feeling words into two categories: positive and negative. The exercise below helps you name more feeling words.

EXERCISE: Naming Feelings

Directions: Fill in five words for each category:

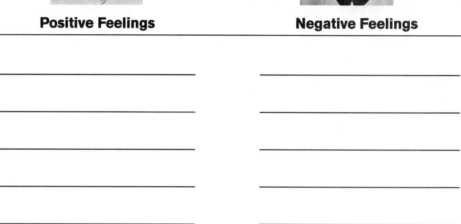

Positive Feelings   **Negative Feelings**

_____   _____

_____   _____

_____   _____

_____   _____

_____   _____

When starting difficult conversations, our focus is on negative or corrective feedback, so we will use feeling words from the negative column. Later when we look at positive feedback, we will use the feeling words from the positive column.

Beware of Loaded Feeling Words

The words you listed in the previous exercise are emotions, which describe how one feels. Often people mistakenly use words other than emotions to express their feelings. These words can cause misunderstandings and lead to more conflict rather than resolution. Here are some examples.

Nonfeeling Words	Interpretation	Better Choice
I want to explode.	You're going to scream and yell.	I feel angry or upset.
I feel violent.	You're going to hit me.	I feel angry or upset.
I feel shut down.	You don't want to hear me.	I feel upset or angry.
I feel edgy.	Say one more thing, and I'll hit you.	I'm irritated.

EXERCISE: Name the Negative Feeling

Part 1

Directions: Below are some descriptions of scenes you might see at work. For each one fill in a negative feeling word that could describe the person's emotions. Use a different word each time.

1. A co-worker comes into work, yanks open the desk drawer, throws his wallet and keys inside, then slams the door.

*Negative feeling word:*_____

2. At the end of the day a co-worker spends a half hour looking for her car keys, which she needs in order to get home.

*Negative feeling word:*_____

3. A friend at work shuffles past you very slowly, mumbles "Hey there," and keeps on walking with his chin on his chest.

*Negative feeling word:*_____

4. A customer pounds his fist on the counter and yells, "I want to see the manager right now!"

*Negative feeling word:*_____

5. A person is the object of a rather personal joke made by someone during a meeting.

*Negative feeling word:*_____

Part 2

Directions: Below are descriptions of events that might happen to you at work. For each one fill in a negative feeling word that might describe your emotions. Use a different word each time.

1. You are not selected for a job you were really hoping for.

*Negative feeling word:*_____

2. Your e-mail system is down and won't let you send messages.

*Negative feeling word:*_____

3. Seven people committed to come to your meeting, but only two showed up.

*Negative feeling word:*_____

4. Co-workers keep teasing you about your new haircut.

*Negative feeling word:*_____

5. One of your co-workers is not doing his part on a project, causing you to miss deadlines, which causes your boss to get upset with you.

*Negative feeling word:*_____

Don't say "I feel like you..."

In the previous step you described the facts regarding another person's behavior. In this step it is important to speak only for yourself, since only you know how you feel. However, we often say, "I feel like you are trying to upset me," instead of "I feel upset." We do this because we are not comfortable describing our personal feelings, so we talk about the other person instead. Saying, "I feel like you..." is an interpretation, and will probably cause an argument. For instance, compare the two statements.

"I feel frustrated."

"I feel like you don't care about me."

The second would probably start an argument, or cause the other person to stop listening. Note the second statement has *you* in it. In this step you should only discuss yourself.

Here are some examples:

Correct:

"I feel angry when you hang up on me."

"I feel hurt that you lied to me."

"I feel frustrated when you keep coming home late."

Incorrect:

"I feel like you're out to get me."

"I feel like I can never trust you again."

"I feel like you're trying to upset me."

"I feel like you..." is an interpretation, not a feeling, and it will often cause an argument.

Also, there are more subtle ways to include "you" and cause the other person to feel attacked. For instance, saying "I feel lied to," implies the other person is a liar. Or saying, "I feel cheated," implies the other person is dishonest. "Lied to" and "cheated" are not emotions or feeling words, and they attack the other person.

Here are some other non-feeling words that attack:

Word	How Used	Implies
cheated	"I feel cheated."	You are a cheat.
lied to	"I feel lied to."	You are a liar.
betrayed	"I feel betrayed."	You are a traitor.
set up	"I feel set up."	You are setting me up.

So what do you say if someone did lie to you or cheat you? If someone did lie to you, how would you feel? Upset? Mad? Angry? Then it is best to say, "When you didn't tell me where you were really going (facts), I felt angry." You have communicated your feelings and stated the facts by describing the behavior that made up the act of lying without using the word "lie." By doing so, you make your point, but you decrease the likelihood that you will make people feel defensive, which will cause them to stop listening to you.

Here is how to replace attacking words with feeling words:

Attacking Words	Feeling Words
"I feel cheated."	"I feel angry."
"I feel lied to."	"I feel upset."
"I feel betrayed."	"I feel furious."
"I feel set up."	"I feel hurt."

Using "Because" Explains Why

Like the person behind you in the movie theater unconsciously kicking your chair, most people do not realize they are doing something to upset you. Frequently people do not understand how their behavior affects you or the organization. That is why it is important to say why you feel the way you do. To tell why, use the word, "because." Here are some examples:

I feel irritated when you interrupt me at meetings *because it breaks my train of thought.*

I feel frustrated when you're late to the meeting *because you don't hear everything, and that makes for inefficient communication.*

I feel angry when you complete your assignments late *because I need your work in order to complete my part of the project.*

I feel irritated when you listen to my phone conversations *because I consider those calls private.*

EXERCISE: Stating Your Feelings

Directions: Below are behaviors that might upset you. Imagine that you have experienced the behavior, and write an "I feel" statement on the right side. (Remember, avoid "I feel like you....") Choose two of the statements and add a "because" phrase.

Situation:	**Feeling:**

Example:
  A friend borrowed money from you and isn't paying you back.

I feel frustrated because I'm depending on that money to pay my bills.

1. A co-worker is frequently late picking you up for work.

_____
_____

2. A relative often calls late at night when you are asleep.

_____
_____

3. Someone sitting next to you in class repeatedly copies your work.

_____
_____

4. A co-worker makes fun of your appearance (clothes, haircut, etc.).

_____
_____

5. Your boss hasn't given you a promised raise.

_____
_____

6. A co-worker often leaves work early, leaving you with extra work.

_____
_____

7. Your co-worker borrows your supplies without asking.

_____
_____

8. Your housemate leaves the dirty dishes in the sink.

_____
_____

HOMEWORK: Feelings or Opinions?

Directions: Read the statements below. If a statement expresses personal feelings and emotions, put an "F" beside it. If a statement uses words that aren't emotions or contains an "I feel like..." phrase, put a "NF" for Not a Feeling.

___ **1.** I feel angry.

___ **2.** I feel uncomfortable about that.

___ **3.** I feel that you care only about yourself.

___ **4.** I'm upset.

___ **5.** I feel you're trying to avoid me.

___ **6.** I feel lied to.

___ **7.** I am disappointed.

___ **8.** I'm irritated by that.

___ **9.** I feel like I want to explode.

___**10.** This makes me crazy!

___**11.** I feel picked on.

___**12.** This is frustrating.

___**13.** I feel you're out to get me.

___**14.** I'm frustrated.

___**15.** I feel dangerous.

State Your Needs

What Do You Want?

Even though **stating your needs** is the fourth step in starting difficult conversations, in some ways it is also the first. When someone upsets you, you want him or her to change that behavior. First, it's important to think about what you want them to do differently. Maybe you want someone to call if he is going to miss a meeting, or to stop making comments about your appearance, or to stop telling you obscene jokes. In any case, you must describe the new behavior in specific, non-blaming words. If you are clear about the behavior you want before you speak, you will be calmer and more confident! Conversely, you are certain to cause conflict if you attack someone's character when you state your needs. Compare these statements:

Behavior:

> I need you to …
>
>> "Clean up after yourself."
>>
>> "Pay me back on time."
>>
>> "Stop commenting on my appearance."

Character:

> I need you to …
>
>> "Stop being a slob."
>>
>> "Not be such a cheat."
>>
>> "Stop being such a pervert."

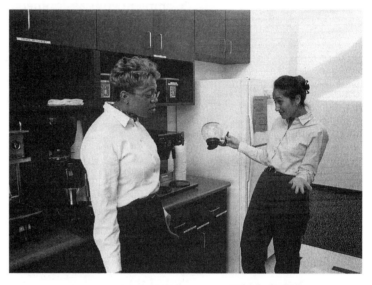

Which describes a behavior and which attacks character?

"When you use the last of the coffee, please refill the pot."

or

"Stop being so inconsiderate."

If you used any of the character statements such as "I need you to stop being such a slob," you are bound to cause a fight because your statement has labeled and insulted someone. But saying, "I need you to return my calls within 24 hours," focuses on behavior. It's what you need, and it isn't a personal attack.

Be Specific

Name the **specific** behavior you want or the other person won't be able to respond. For instance, try responding to the following requests:

"Get a clue!"

"Wake up and smell the coffee."

"Get with the program."

"Get your act together."

versus

"Listen to me without interrupting."

"Spend within your budget."

"Be on time for your appointments."

"Complete your assignments on time."

Specific requests help people understand what you want. They may not necessarily give it to you, but at least you have spoken clearly and played fair. You know what you need, and if they can't help you, perhaps someone else can.

Other Ways to Say "I need..."

Starting your need statement with "I need" can sometimes sound too demanding or abrupt. Here are some other words to help you describe the behavior you are looking for.

"What I'd like…"

"So would you please…"

"I'd prefer it if…"

"So I'm asking you to…"

You Can Focus On Outcomes

Sometimes saying, "I need you to..." seems too direct. A less forceful way to state your needs is by focusing on the outcome. You describe what you would like to see changed. For instance, suppose that your neighbor's dog barks at night, keeping you awake. You approach the neighbor and describe the facts and your feelings, such as, "The last two weeks Sparky has barked until 3 a.m. It's frustrating for me, because I can't sleep."

Here are two different ways to state your needs:

"I need you to get Sparky to stop barking."

"I need it quiet after 10 p.m. so I can sleep."

The first approach tells your neighbor what you want him or her to do. The second describes the situation if the problem were fixed. There is no correct answer. Each approach has advantages and disadvantages, and you should know what they are before you use them.

The first approach, using an "I need you to..." is a directive and describes the behavior that you want to see. Because it describes the behavior specifically, it leaves less room for interpretation or misunderstanding. It is useful when someone doesn't know the behavior that you expect. However, it is a fairly assertive approach.

The second approach, describing the ideal outcome, is less direct and focuses on results, rather than a specific behavior. It is a subtle way of saying, "Here's the result I want. How can we solve this problem?" However, because it is less direct, it leaves more room for interpretation. It can also be used improperly. If you use this approach to avoid direct confrontation, you might be so vague that the other person does not understand what you want.

The best guideline for choosing either of these approaches is to know your audience and the situation.

EXERCISE: Good Needs Statements?

Directions: Below are some "needs statements." Under each statement put a check mark next to either the correct or incorrect way to make a needs statement. If it is incorrect, briefly state why.

1. I need you to get with it.
___ Correct   ___ Incorrect Why?_____

2. I need you to not yell at the customers.
___ Correct   ___ Incorrect Why?_____

3. I need someone I can count on.
___ Correct   ___ Incorrect Why?_____

4. I need you to stop being so selfish.
___ Correct   ___ Incorrect Why?_____

5. You need to get a better attitude.
___ Correct   ___ Incorrect Why?_____

6. So please write down all of my phone messages.
___ Correct   ___ Incorrect Why?_____

7. I need headquarters to receive the reports by the 15th of every month.
___ Correct   ___ Incorrect Why?_____

8. I'd like the cash register receipts calculated every evening.
___ Correct   ___ Incorrect Why?_____

9. So would you please store the delivery truck keys in the safe at night.
___ Correct   ___ Incorrect Why?_____

10. I need you to be a better communicator.
___ Correct   ___ Incorrect Why?_____

EXERCISE: Stating Your Needs

Directions: Below are descriptions of some upsetting behaviors. They are the same behaviors you wrote feelings statements for on page 61. In the space next to the description write the different behavior or the outcome you would like to see.

Situation:	**Need:**

Example:
A friend borrowed money from you and isn't paying it back.

I need you to pay me back by Friday.

1. A co-worker is frequently late picking you up for work.

_____
_____

2. A relative often calls late at night when you are asleep.

_____
_____

3. Someone sitting next to you in class repeatedly copies your work.

_____
_____

4. A co-worker makes fun of your appearance (clothes, haircut, etc.).

_____
_____

5. Your boss hasn't given you a promised raise.

_____
_____

6. A co-worker often leaves work early, leaving you with extra work.

_____
_____

7. Your co-worker borrows your supplies without asking.

_____
_____

8. Your housemate leaves the dirty dishes in the sink.

_____
_____

Ask for a Response

Show That You Are Open

The final step in starting a difficult conversation is to **ask the other person for a response** to what you've said. By asking for a response you show you are open to hearing the other person's viewpoints, which invites cooperation.

Saying something like, "What do you think?" invites a response and shows you are open. Notice how the woman is using her hands to invite a response.

Some good examples of this step are:

"What do you think?"

"Okay?"

"What's your view?"

"What's your reaction?"

Any of these questions invite a response.

Sometimes Stronger Is Better

On occasion, you need a stronger closing that doesn't ask for an opinion. You might find yourself in a situation where someone has done something so upsetting that negotiating seems ridiculous. For example, someone calls you an extremely insulting name. Examples of stronger closings would be:

"Is that clear?"

"Got it?"

"All right?"

However, be careful with such forceful endings, and consider your audience. Such closings might work with a friend or co-worker who understands you well, but you probably would not use them on your boss.

Sometimes you need to be very direct and say something like, "Is that clear?" Notice how assertive the man on the left appears by pointing.

EXERCISE: Soft/Firm Closings

Directions: There are two ways to close your start to a difficult conversation, depending on the situation: soft/asking or firm/telling. List several of each.

Soft/Asking	Firm/Telling
Example:	
What do you think?	*Is that clear?*
1. _____	_____
2. _____	_____
3. _____	_____

Putting It All Together

Following is an example of all five steps of starting a difficult conversation:

Check: "Hey Nick, can I talk to you about something important?"

Facts: "Last week you borrowed my tools without asking."

Feelings: "I felt angry when you did that because I couldn't complete a hot customer order."

Needs: "I'm willing to lend you my tools, but I need you to ask first."

Ask: "Okay?"

EXERCISE: Practice with Starting Difficult Conversations

Directions: Imagine that you have a problem with someone, and you have to open a difficult conversation about it. Write down what you might say, following the Check, Facts, Feelings, Needs, Ask format.

PROBLEM 1

Alex, a co-worker, frequently listens in on your phone conversations. When you hang up he asks you questions like, "So your kids are having trouble in school, huh?" Tell Alex you need privacy when you are making calls.

Check:

Facts:

Feelings:

Needs:

Ask:

PROBLEM 2

Your boss is a smoker, and smoke really bothers you. You have to share an office, and there are no windows. You haven't said anything because you like the job, but you have decided that you can't stand the smoke anymore. Write down what you would say to your boss.

Check:

Facts:

Feelings:

Needs:

Ask:

PROBLEM ❸

You pay the phone bill and your roommate is supposed to pay the utility bill, but he often forgets. Twice, the utility company has cut off your power because of non-payment, and they're threatening to do it again. You're tired of being cold and in the dark. Write down what you would say to your roommate.

Check:

Facts:

Feelings:

Needs:

Ask:

PROBLEM 4

You are working on a project with Dave, a co-worker. Dave has been late completing some of his tasks, which you need in order to complete some of your parts of the project. You are concerned that Dave's missed deadlines are going to cause the project to fall behind schedule, which will make you look bad. Write down what you would say to Dave regarding the need for him to complete his work on time.

Check:

Facts:

Feelings:

Needs:

Ask:

HOMEWORK: How Are These Statements?

Directions: Below are several examples of starts to difficult conversations. Each uses the five steps discussed earlier: Check, Facts, Feelings, Needs, Ask. In four of them at least one step is incorrect. One of them is completely correct. Read each statement, identify the incorrect step(s), and write a few words about what is wrong with it. If you think the statement is completely correct, write "all correct" in the space provided.

Example: "Tony, can we talk for a minute? I noticed you borrowed my laptop computer over the weekend without letting me know. It was frustrating for me because I didn't know where it was. So get a clue and get your own. All right?"

What's wrong: Need statement attacks Tony, and it is too vague.

1. "Hey John, do you have a minute to talk? I noticed you were late to the staff meeting today. It's frustrating when you are not there. You really need to be more considerate of others and show up on time like the rest of us. What are your thoughts?

What's wrong: _____

_____

2. "Tiffany, can I talk with you for a minute? The software program you wrote is pretty messed up. It's irritating because I expected it to work correctly. I need the program to calculate payroll for the entire year. How can we get this fixed?"

What's wrong: _____

_____

3. "Maria, can I talk with you privately? You are setting a bad example for the less experienced members of the department. It's frustrating to me because they look up to you for guidance as to how to conduct themselves. Please be more of a team player. Can we work this out?"

What's wrong: _____

_____

4. "Lydia, do you have a few minutes? Twice in the meeting today you interrupted me. It's frustrating when you do that because I'm not able to contribute my ideas completely. I want to hear your input, but I also need you to let me finish when I'm speaking. Can we work this out?"

What's wrong: _____

_____

5. "Erica, may we talk privately for a minute? I don't think you are helping much with the new sales project. I feel upset about it because you know a lot about sales and we could benefit from your knowledge. I would like to see that we get more of your input about our strategy. How can we work this out?"

What's wrong: _____

_____

EXERCISE: Real-Life Problems

Directions: Here are problems that many of us encounter every day. Read each problem, then think how you would use the five steps to address them. In the blank spaces provided, write out what you would say to each person.

PROBLEM ❶

I've worked for the same boss for the last two years. Our company is using computers more every day. I want to take several computer classes to keep my skills current. I've asked my boss several times if I could attend some classes, but each time he says we're too busy or there isn't enough money. However, since then he's sent other people to the classes, including some new employees. This doesn't seem fair. I want to talk to him about this, but it's not easy. How do I bring it up?

Check:

Facts:

Feelings:

Needs:

Ask:

PROBLEM 2

My friend and I opened a coffee bar a year ago. Business is good, but something has happened lately that bothers me. As you can imagine, some of our customers are very picky about their coffee. They want their steamed milk frothy, not runny; or the coffee is too cold, or too weak. When customers complain to my partner, David will fix the problem, but he gets visibly upset. He slams things around and is gruff with the customers, not saying much and just sort of glaring at them. I'm worried because if we scare off our customers, we'll never be as big as Starbuck's. How should I approach him about this problem?

Check:

Facts:

Feelings:

Needs:

Ask:

PROBLEM ③

My neighbor likes to fix old cars, and he works on them in his garage. Sometimes he works late at night and runs an engine really loud. The noise keeps me awake, and I have to go to work early. How should I approach him?

Check:

Facts:

Feelings:

Needs:

Ask:

PROBLEM ④

I have a computer at my desk at work. A co-worker likes to use it while I am at lunch. She will often leave my desk area really messy when she's done. She eats lunch and stains some of my work with crumbs or soft drink spills. I don't mind her using my computer. I'm just tired of how inconsiderate she is about the mess she makes. I know she would be upset if I did the same to her work area. How do I bring this up?

Check:

Facts:

Feelings:

Needs:

Ask:

HOMEWORK: Think of Other Difficult Situations

Directions: Think of five real-life problems that you've experienced or seen happen to someone, problems that require starting a difficult conversation. Write a couple of sentences to describe each one. Then choose one of the problems for which you'll write your own five-step response (Check, Facts, Feelings, Needs, Ask).

Five Problems

1._____

_____

_____

2._____

_____

_____

3._____

_____

_____

4._____

_____

_____

5._____

_____

_____

Name:_____

HOMEWORK: Think of Other Difficult Situations

Directions: Select one of the five problems you listed on the previous page and write out what you would say to start a conversation about it.

Situation:_____

_____

_____

Check: _____

_____

_____

Facts: _____

_____

_____

Feelings: _____

_____

_____

Needs: _____

_____

_____

Ask: _____

_____

_____

"Playing Jazz"—Improvising in Difficult Conversations

You may have found yourself saying, "But I don't talk like that," as you worked through the previous sections on starting difficult conversations. The three major steps—facts, feelings, needs—are a framework. You do not have to use them exactly as you have studied them so far. In this section you will learn a variety of ways to use these three steps to start difficult conversations.

Think of a group of jazz musicians performing on a stage. No one uses written music. Throughout the performance the musicians improvise on a theme. As they perform, there are times when someone plays solo, and other times when they perform together. What they play changes often, depending on their skill levels, what they heard, who they are playing with, or the mood of the audience. In order to improvise, each musician must be well schooled in music fundamentals. In fact, many jazz musicians have extensive backgrounds in the fundamentals, such as classical music. Even though they improvise during performances, their daily practice routines are based on foundation skills, such as playing scales.

A jazz musician improvises, but the improvisation is based on fundamentals. Improvising difficult conversations works the same way.

The same is true for the skill of starting difficult conversations. In real life when you use this skill, you will be improvising, depending on the situation. Who you are talking to, what you're discussing, and where you are discussing it will all play into what you say. In other words, like jazz musicians, you will be improvising just about every time you start a difficult conversation. However, what you say is based on the fundamental steps of facts, feelings, and needs, just as the jazz musician's performance is based on fundamental musical skills.

Here are some ways that you can improvise the skill of starting difficult conversations.

1. Drop the need statement (fact, feeling).

Sometimes the need is obvious, and you don't need to state it.

> "When you show up late (*fact*), I feel frustrated (*feeling*)."

It is obvious you're asking the person to show up on time, so dropping the need statement works here.

People often use this version when talking to a boss, because they do not want to tell the boss what to do.

"My performance review is three months late (*fact*), and I feel frustrated about that (*feeling*)."

2. Drop the need statement and switch fact and feeling (feeling, fact).

Again, this statement can be used when the need is obvious, but you suspect the person you are dealing with is more feelings-oriented, and will respond better to the effect the behavior is having on you.

> "I feel so frustrated (*feeling*), when you show up late (*fact*)."

> "I feel frustrated (*feeling*), that my performance review is three months late (*fact*)."

3. Drop the feelings (fact, need).

Sometimes you or the person you are talking to is not comfortable discussing feelings. So drop the feeling statement. Remember, most of our messages are sent through nonverbal communications, so the way you say something can have the same effect as an "I feel" statement.

> (Looking and sounding frustrated) "This is the third time your department has been late with the project (*facts*), and I need to see a plan put in place so this will not happen again (*needs*)."

4. Use feelings without using the "feel" word.

Sometimes you want to include your feelings, but you know that if the other person hears the word "feel" he will stop listening or get defensive for whatever reason. So just drop the "feel" word.

> "I'm frustrated…"
>
> "It's frustrating…"
>
> "This is frustrating…"

5. State the facts, then check them out.

Suppose you aren't absolutely sure of the facts. Start with what you think the facts are, then ask for a response. It might sound like this:

> "Sue, I haven't seen you in the mornings several times this week. Tell me why that is."

Depending on the response, add feelings and needs. For instance, Sue might say, "Yes, I've been coming in late because I have friends visiting from out-of-town and we've been staying out late." Then you respond with feelings and needs such as, "When you're not here, it frustrates your customers, so please be in by 8:30 at the latest."

Sometimes the other person will deny the facts, even though you know they are true. If neither of you can prove your facts, you do not want to fall into an endless argument of, "Yes you did!" "No I didn't!" But you *can* make a statement that will prevent the behavior from happening again. Here is how it works.

You suspect that Joe is leaving work early, but you're not sure. You start the conversation with a, "facts, check it out" statement.

> "Hey Joe twice this week I couldn't find you after four o'clock. Why was that?"

> "Oh, I was in the warehouse checking inventory."

You are pretty sure this is a lie, but you cannot prove it. So you respond with the following:

> "Oh, okay. Well, in the future would you let me know when you are going to be away from your desk, so I know where to find you?"

> "Yeah, sure."

You did not prove Joe a liar, but you did request behavior that will stop him from disappearing in the future. In this type of situation that may be the best outcome you can hope for.

Improvising Has Its Limits

While jazz musicians improvise what they play onstage, there are certain rules they do not violate. For instance, a musician would not play out of key or at a different tempo from the other musicians. The same is true with starting difficult conversations. There are certain ways in which the three steps—facts, feelings, needs—should not be used.

Here are some ways **not** to improvise starting difficult conversations, no matter what the situation.

1. Don't Drop the Facts

Even if someone did something to you just two seconds ago, you need to name the behavior. Often people are not aware of their behavior, and if you don't describe it they might not be aware of it. In the different ways to improvise listed previously, each one included the facts.

If you don't include the facts, people often respond with, "Can you give me some specifics?" So you will be providing the facts anyway. Why not give the facts up front, and avoid the problem of defensiveness? Here is how a conversation might go if you leave out the facts.

> "I feel frustrated (*feeling*), and I need you to start showing up on time (*need*)."
>
> "What do you mean? When have I been late?"
>
> "Last Wednesday, this Thursday..."

2. Don't Start with the Needs

If you start with a need statement, people do not have a context (the facts), so they will probably stop listening to you. In addition, starting a difficult conversation with "You need" sounds dictatorial, and some people get defensive or stubborn if they feel they are being told what to do.

Compare the tone of these two statements.

> "I need you to get here on time (*need*). It's frustrating (*feeling*) when you are late (*fact*)."
>
> It's frustrating (*feeling*) when you are late (*fact*). I need you to get here on time (*need*)."

Exercise: Improvise These Difficult Conversations

Directions: Below are situations that you addressed earlier using the five steps of starting difficult conversations. Now take the same situations and improvise them. Each exercise asks you to improvise in a different way.

Example: Every Wednesday at 2:00 you have a meeting with a co-worker. Frequently he is at least fifteen minutes late. Once again he just walked into your office, late. You are frustrated; you don't feel respected, and you want the meeting to start on time. Address this issue with your co-worker.

Improvise by: *Dropping the need statement, since it is obvious what you need.*

1. Check: "Tony, can I talk with you for a minute?"
2. Fact: "When you are late like this."
3. Feeling: "I feel frustrated."
4. Ask: "How can we work this out?"

1. Alex, a co-worker, frequently listens in on your phone conversations. When you hang up he asks you questions like, "So your kids are having trouble in school, huh?" Tell Alex you need privacy when you are making calls.

Improvise by: Starting with your feelings first, then the facts.

Check: _____

Feeling: _____

Facts: _____

Needs: _____

Ask: _____

2. Your boss is a smoker, and smoke really bothers you. You have to share an office, and there are no windows. You haven't said anything because you like the job, but you have decided that you can't stand smoke anymore. Write what you would say to your boss.

Improvise by: Dropping the need statement, since you don't want your boss to think you are telling him or her what to do.

Check: _____

Facts: _____

Feeling: _____

Ask: _____

3. You pay the phone bill and your roommate is supposed to pay the utility bill, but he forgets. Twice the utility company has cut off your power because of the nonpayment, and they are threatening to do it again. You are tired of being cold and in the dark. Write down what you would say to your roommate.

Improvise by: Dropping the feeling statement, and briefly describe how you would act to convey your feelings to your roommate.

Check: _____

Facts: _____

Needs: _____

Ask: _____

How would you act to convey your feelings: _____

_____

4. You are working on a project with Dave, a co-worker. Dave has been late completing some of his tasks, which you need in order to complete your part of the project. You are concerned that Dave's missed deadlines will cause the project to fall behind schedule, which will make you look bad. Write down what you would say to Dave about your need for him to complete his work on time.

Improvise by: Using a feeling statement without using the words, "I feel..."

Check: _____

Facts: _____

Feeling: _____

Needs: _____

Ask: _____

5. You have a co-worker who tries to listen in on your personal phone calls. When you are on a personal call, he starts working at the computer right next to the phone, even though other computers are available. In addition, he rarely uses the computer, unless you are on the phone. You are not sure he is listening in, but when you glance his way he does not seem to be working. Also, he has asked questions about your personal life that you considered invasive.

This exercise has two parts:

Part 1: Improvise by: Using the "facts, check it out" method to address this.

Your "state the facts, check it out" statement:

_____

_____

Part 2: Suppose your co-worker will not admit that he is listening to your calls. His answer to your "facts, check it out" statement is:

"Oh I just use the computer whenever I have a chance. It's just a coincidence that you are on the phone when I use it."

Respond to his reply with a request that will keep him from listening to your calls again.

Your request for the future: _____

_____

Providing Positive Feedback

"Feedback" is a word often associated with criticism. When someone says, "I'd like to give you some feedback," we often have feelings of unease or dread, and we wonder, "What did I do wrong?"

We feel this way because people often give negative feedback incorrectly. They don't know how to start difficult conversations, so they attack, blame, or use the words "always" and "never."

A second reason feedback gets a bad name is that we hear more negative feedback than positive. Have you ever found yourself saying, "I only hear about things when I mess up"? One reason is that people find positive feedback almost as diffficult to give as negative feedback.

We feel uncomfortable giving positive feedback for several reasons:

- We don't want to sound like a cheerleader "rah-rah" type.
- We are afraid we will embarrass the other person with a compliment.
- We don't know what to say, other than "good job."

Providing positive feedback is a skill, and knowing how to use it can overcome the fears listed above. In this section you will learn how to give positive feedback. The skills are essentially the same as those in the chapter, Starting Difficult Conversations. Anyone can provide another person with positive feedback, not just the boss. Used properly, positive feedback has many benefits in the workplace. Among them are:

- Creates stronger relationships with co-workers
- Improves team performance
- Builds trust among team members

To provide positive feedback:

1. Check the timing.

2. State the facts.

3. State your feelings, or the positive effect the behavior has had on you.

4. State your needs or encourage more positive behavior (optional).

5. Close with thanks.

Here's a brief look at each step.

Check the timing

Whether you're starting a difficult conversation or providing positive feedback, it is wise to find out if the person is ready to hear it. Positive feedback delivered at the wrong time could have a detrimental effect. For instance, some people prefer private appreciation over public praise. If you can, find out first how the person prefers to hear praise.

Examples:

> "Hey John, I would like to say thanks for something. Do you have a minute?"

> "Christy, may I talk to you for a minute about the great job you did on the project?"

> "Janet, I want to give you some appreciative feedback. Do you have a minute?"

Notice how in each of these statements the speaker indicated that positive feedback was coming. This helps to put others at ease right away.

State the facts

For this step, the rules for starting difficult conversations apply to positive feedback: state the facts, and be specific. As with difficult conversations, mere opinions or vagueness can lead to misunderstandings.

Correct examples:

> "You processed that urgent order in less than a half hour."

> "You explained our products thoroughly to that new customer."

> "You reduced our copier repair costs by more than ten thousand dollars."

Incorrect examples:

> "You are amazing!"

> "You made all the right moves with that customer."

> "You've got what it takes to help this company."

> "You're the best!"

The correct examples describe specific behaviors. The incorrect examples, while meant to be complimentary, were vague. They did not tell the person what he or she had done well.

State your feelings, or the effect of a behavior

Explaining the positive effect of someone's behavior is very powerful. It provides background, and tells him or her exactly how they helped you or the company.

Examples:

> "When you gave me the report a half-hour early, I was able to review it before I met with the boss (*facts*). I really appreciated that because I was prepared to answer her tough questions (*feelings/effect*)."

> "Thanks for reminding me that the new drill presses were due for maintenance (*facts*). I really appreciated that because I would have forgotten, and you helped avoid some expensive repair bills (*feelings/effect*)."

State your needs or encourage more positive behavior

This step is not always necessary when providing positive feedback, but it does encourage continued positive results.

Examples:

> "Although it's not required, I always appreciate your getting the report here early. I can never be too prepared to meet with the boss."

> "If you see any other maintenance issues I'm forgetting, don't hesitate to let me know again. Thanks!"

Close with thanks

Closing with some short comment of appreciation is always nice, and it is appropriate for positive feedback.

Examples:

> "So thanks, and keep up the good work."
> "I sure appreciate your efforts."
> "Thanks again for your thoughtfulness."

Exercise: Provide Positive Feedback

Directions: Below are some brief descriptions of positive behaviors you might experience in the workplace. For each, provide positive feedback using the steps discussed previously.

Example:

You are out sick for several days right before you are supposed to ship an important order, and a co-worker finishes the job for you.

Check: *"Hey Kerry, do you have a minute for me to say thank you for something?*
Facts: *I came back this morning after being out sick and found the Whitson order had shipped on time.*
Feelings/effect: *I really appreciate your help because it would have been late, and they are one of our most important customers.*
Encourage: *That kind of teamwork makes our department look good.*
Closing: *So thanks. I really appreciate your initiative."*

1. You work the night shift. Your counterpart on the day shift leaves you a detailed note each night about what happened, including problems that occurred and what work remains for you to complete.

Check _____

Facts _____

Feeling/effect _____

Encourage (optional) _____

Closing _____

2. Several times a month, without being asked, your office receptionist comes by and asks if you want him to order any office supplies for you.

Check _____

Facts _____

Feeling/effect _____

Encourage (optional) _____

Closing _____

---

3. You called in sick one day. A co-worker covered for you at a scheduled meeting with an important customer, and made a sale for you.

Check _____

Facts _____

Feeling/effect _____

Encourage (optional) _____

Closing _____

4. You own a restaurant. You watched one of your waiters handle a customer who was upset about slow service. The waiter expedited the customer's order and gave him a reasonable discount (which was okay with you). The customer left happy and paid the waiter a compliment for handling the situation.

Check _____

Facts _____

Feeling/effect _____

Encourage (optional) _____

Closing _____

5. On her own, one of your employees designed a Web site for your company that has attracted a lot of new customers.

Check _____

Facts _____

Feeling/effect _____

Encourage (optional) _____

Closing _____

Active Listening

Using More Than Your Ears

What part of your body do you use to listen? If you said your ears, you are partially correct. To listen well you actually use your whole body: your eyes, hands, mouth, face, mind, and heart.

When was the last time you felt like someone wasn't listening to you? Maybe she was reading the paper or watching TV while you talked. Even though she might have heard your words, you didn't feel listened to because her actions told you that she was interested in something else.

Active listening means using your body *and* your words to show your interest. Listening is one of the most important communication tools you will ever use. In this section, you will learn to use words and body language to listen well.

You use MUCH more than your ears to listen.

Facts and Feelings: The Most Important Parts of Communication

When we communicate we usually send a two-part message: one is the facts, the other is our feelings about the facts. Every message—whether spoken, written, or non-verbal—is based on facts, or feelings, or both.

Facts are generally communicated with words. **Feelings** are communicated that way too, but they are also communicated with body language, tone of voice, and gestures. To understand someone fully, you must listen actively to *both* facts and feelings. Here are some examples of facts and feelings in words or actions:

Facts:

"The bus comes at 7:15."

"I lost my wallet."

"I got fired."

Feeling Words:

"I'm scared."

"I feel angry!"

"I'm so mad!"

Feeling Actions:

Clenched fists

Smiles

Tears

In this section you will learn to identify both facts and feelings in the communications you receive from others. This skill is critical since the communication techniques you learn in the rest of the book depend on an ability to identify facts and feelings.

When he says, "This tree is 50 years old," this man is communicating only facts.

This man is communicating feelings in words and actions when he says, "I feel great!"

Rolling your eyes communicates feelings with actions, not words.

Facts Cause Feelings

What are some of the little things that bother you? A guy uses the express line at the grocery store even though he has far more than ten items. You wake up late because you set your alarm clock for 7:00 p.m. instead of 7:00 a.m. A woman saves the best seats at the movie theater for her friends, who arrive just before the show starts. Your computer crashes and you lose two hours of work.

Now consider some of the little things that you appreciate—things that make you feel good. Someone stops so you can cross a busy street. The instructional manual with your new computer explains perfectly how to set it up. The telephone repair man arrives on time.

In each example above, your feelings—positive or negative—were caused by some action. It is actions that cause feelings, and those actions are called **the facts.**

The key point here is that **people have feelings about facts**. Sometimes people communicate just the facts, other times just the feelings, and sometimes both facts and feelings. Being able to separate and identify these two parts is a very powerful skill.

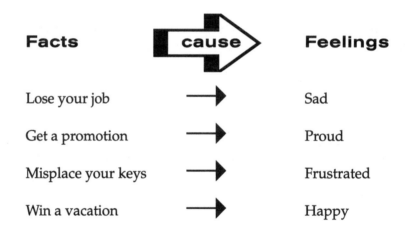

Facts	cause	Feelings
Lose your job	→	Sad
Get a promotion	→	Proud
Misplace your keys	→	Frustrated
Win a vacation	→	Happy

Facts and Feelings

Following are examples of facts and feelings that show how we use them to communicate.

Your friend and co-worker, Nick, walks up to you in the lunch room and says sourly, "My boss, Alan, just left the company, and they just promoted Mark Smith to be my new boss! He is so incompetent! I can't believe they chose him." He rolls his eyes, shakes his head, flings his soda can into the trash, and stomps away.

In this example, Nick used words to communicate the clear facts of the situation, but you would be a poor listener if you didn't pick up on his strong feelings. Nick was probably both angry and very frustrated. Active listening skills provide awareness of the emotion in Nick's face, gestures, and tone of voice.

Here is another example. Suppose you sneak in the back door at work two hours late only to find your boss waiting for you.

"I'm so angry at you! You're two hours late and we're swamped with customers!" She then slams her fist on the counter and glares at you.

In this case, your boss used words to communicate the facts. You were two hours late. What are your boss's feelings? Were they communicated with words or with actions? The answer is both! Your boss said she was "angry," and drove the message home with her facial expression and her gestures.

EXERCISE: Identifying Facts and Feelings

Directions: Facts are communicated with words, and feelings are communicated with words and/or actions. This exercise provides practice in spotting both. Write the facts and feelings expressed in each situation.

Example:
Juan says, "We're having an earthquake!" He looks around wildly and dives under a table.

Facts: There's an earthquake.

Feelings: Scared

1. Calla says, "When you borrow my car without asking, I feel frustrated."

Facts:_____

Feelings: _____

2. Don yells, "This meeting is a waste of time!" He storms out of the room.

Facts: _____

Feelings: _____

3. Sarah states, "The blue whale is the largest animal on earth."

Facts:_____

Feelings: _____

4. Ali shouts, "This is the third time you've been late!"

Facts:_____

Feelings: _____

HOMEWORK: Is It Facts, Feelings, or Both?

Directions: Below are ten short statements. For each one, decide if the statement contains facts, feelings, or both. Put a check in the column that corresponds to your answer.

	Facts	**Feelings**	**Both**
Example: "It's 7:30," said Jim.	✓	_____	_____
1. "I've had it!" snapped Mona.	_____	_____	_____
2. "Only a one percent raise?" exclaimed Rob.	_____	_____	_____
3. "What is with you?" growled Eddie.	_____	_____	_____
4. "I'm the oldest of five children," said Anna.	_____	_____	_____
5. "I got a promotion!" shouted Antonio.	_____	_____	_____
6. "I can't take this anymore!" shrieked Lamont.	_____	_____	_____
7. "Oh please!" said Mark as he rolled his eyes.	_____	_____	_____
8. "This shirt is stained," said Bill.	_____	_____	_____
9. "The computer is down again!" howled Stan.	_____	_____	_____
10. "I'm allergic to milk products," said Martha.	_____	_____	_____

HOMEWORK: Feelings Through Words, Actions, or Both?

Directions: All of the statements below contain feelings. Some feelings are communicated with words, some with actions, and some with both. Check the column that describes how the feelings are communicated. In the last column name or describe the feeling.

	Words	Actions	Both	Feeling?
Example: *"You scratched my car!"* *shouted Latoya.*		✓		mad
1. Alejandro slammed the door.				
2. "I'm so frustrated! You're late again!" she yelled.				
3. "What a lousy day," muttered Kristen.				
4. "Look at this report!" bellowed the boss.				
5. "When you lie to me I feel hurt," she said through tears.				
6. "Be quiet!" shouted Juanita.				
7. "I can't believe this!" Peter groaned.				
8. "Nice job," said the boss, smiling.				
9. "That's it!" Ryan shouted and stalked away.				
10. "I'm afraid to ride with you when you drink!" Amy cried.				

Simple Signals

Signals That Show You Are Listening

A traffic signal tells you when to go, and when to stop. When you are with someone, you also send signals that tell when you are listening, and when you are not.

To let someone know that you are listening, send simple signals that you're interested. **Simple signals** are actions or words. They are easy to send, and you already know many of them. Simple signals are very useful tools whether you are receiving facts or feelings from someone.

Simple signal actions:

- Look at the other person.
- Turn away from the computer.
- Nod.
- Turn off your cell phone.

Simple signal words:

- "Uh-huh."
- "Tell me more."
- "Really?"
- "Oh, wow!"

Just as a traffic signal tells you to stop or go, simple signals send a message about whether or not you are listening.

Is the man on the left getting a simple signal that the man on the right is listening?

"Tell Me More..." Helps in Difficult Situations

One of the more powerful simple signals is "tell me more...." It is useful in many situations to get more information, give you time to think, and diffuse accusations. Here's how it works.

Provides More Information

Bob is talking as he is walking toward you. He is upset and he's not making a lot of sense. You don't know how to react. You don't want to say, "I have no idea what you're talking about." That might embarrass or upset him even more. Simply saying, "Tell me more about that," keeps him talking and gives you more information without being combative.

Gives You Time to Think

You are caught off guard by the angry approach of a co-worker. You don't know how to respond. Simply saying something like, "Can you tell me a little bit more about the situation?" gives you precious seconds to gather your wits.

Diffuses Accusations

Martha makes an accusation about you. Rather than getting defensive or angry you deflect the anger, give yourself time to think, and force her to back up the accusation with proof by saying something like, "Tell me why you feel that way...." or "What makes you say that?"

Other Ways of Saying, "Tell Me More."

> "What's up?"
> "What's happening?"
> "What's going on?"
> "Say more about that."

_____

_____

_____

EXERCISE: Listening Practice

Directions: Sit with a partner and listen to him or her talk for one minute about any topic. If you can't think of a topic here are some ideas:

- What do you think the new millennium will bring?
- What do you think about legalizing drugs?
- What do you think about this class?

Use simple signals to let your partner know you are interested. What signals did you use?

Actions

- _____
- _____
- _____

Words

- _____
- _____
- _____

HOMEWORK: Simple Signals

Directions: Describe two examples of people using good simple listening signals, and two examples of bad listening signals. They can be from your life, others around you, or from television. Describe who you were watching and what the signals were.

Good Simple Signals

Example:
Person: My friend
Location: At work
Good Signals: Ignored the ringing phone while I was talking to her.

1. Person _____

   Location _____

   Good Signals _____

2. Person _____

   Location _____

   Good Signals _____

Bad Simple Signals

Example:
Person: Family member
Location: At home
Bad Signals: Kept watching TV while I was talking to him.

1. Person _____

   Location _____

   Bad Signals _____

2. Person _____

   Location _____

   Bad Signals _____

Mirroring—
Understanding Feelings

When people have strong feelings, those feelings are *about* something. That something is what someone said or did, in other words, *facts*. **People have feelings about facts!** Look at the following examples:

"I'm upset (*feeling*) that you are late (*fact*)."

"I've had it with you (*feeling*) for lying to me (*fact*)."

I'm tired (*feeling*) of lending you money (*fact*)."

In these examples the feelings were caused by the facts. But people do not always tell us the facts; they just rush at us with feelings, like the following statements.

"I'm so upset!"

"I've had it with you!"

"I'm tired of this!"

To understand a problem, you must discover the facts that are causing the feelings. You can do this with a technique called **mirroring**.

Holding Up the Mirror

Mirroring works like this: imagine you are holding a small mirror in front of you. Who do you see? Yourself. Now turn the mirror around and hold it facing someone else. Who does he see? Himself! Mirroring is a method for letting someone know you understand his feelings by telling him what emotions you see. It sounds simple, but you'll find it a powerful tool that makes people feel listened to and understood.

Mirroring uses short phrases to reflect a person's emotions back to him or her.

When you hold up a mirror like this, you see yourself.

Three common mirroring phrases are:

- "You look…"
- "You seem…"
- "You sound…"

Examples:

- "You look sad."
- "You seem frustrated."
- "You sound upset."

The last one, "you sound…," is very effective for people who do a lot of phone work.

Once people know you understand their feelings, you can deal with the facts. It sounds simple, but it is amazing how often reflecting feelings to someone makes them feel understood, which calms them. When they calm down, they will begin to tell you the facts behind their feelings.

When you hold up a mirror like this, the other person sees what you see. Mirroring is telling someone what you see with words like, "You seem upset."

Mirror Feelings to Get to the Facts

Think of conflict as an onion. At the center of the onion is the resolution of a conflict, or some sort of agreement. But surrounding the center are layers of facts, which are covered by layers of feelings. The outer peelings of the onion, the feelings, are often what we encounter first when there is conflict. In order to get a resolution, we must peel away the feelings first to get to the facts, which we hope will lead to a resolution. Mirroring helps because *people have feelings about facts.*

If we mirror feelings with short statements like, "You look…" or "You seem…" they will feel understood and begin to tell us the facts about their feelings, which helps us reach a resolution. At times you do not even need to get to the facts; sometimes people just want to vent their feelings. If they feel you understand their feelings, they will calm down.

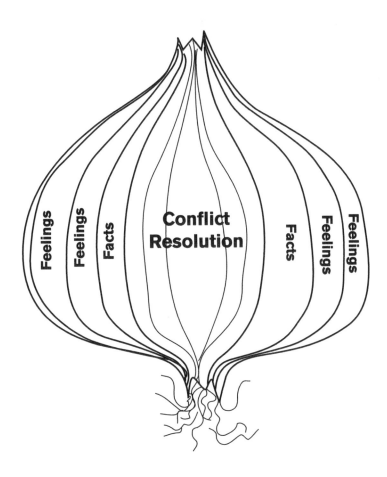

Think of conflict as an onion.
Mirroring helps you peel away feelings
to get facts, which can lead to resolution.

Here are a few examples of how reflecting back feelings helps get to the facts.

> Terri and Mark are co-workers. Terri approaches Mark in the hallway looking very agitated.
>
> Terri: "There you are! You've got a lot of nerve!"
>
> Mark: "Wow, you seem really upset (*mirrors*). What's the matter?" (*Tell me more.*)
>
> Terri: "You were supposed to give me the report by nine o'clock! That was two hours ago! Now I'm going to be late giving it to the boss all because of you! "

When Terri first approached, Mark did not have any information about why Terri was irritated. By mirroring her feelings of anger, "You seem really upset," and by using a "tell me more" statement, "What's the matter?" Terri began to give Mark the facts—that she believed he was late with the report.

> A customer calls the customer service line of a catalog company.
>
> Service representative: "Top Line Sporting Wear. How may I help you?"
>
> Customer: "I have had it with your company!" he barks into the phone.
>
> Service representative: "You sound very upset, sir (*mirrors*). What is the problem?" (*Tell me more.*)
>
> Customer: "I ordered a snow parka three weeks ago, and it's not here. I'm leaving on a ski trip today, and I don't have a parka because of your lousy service."

When the customer service representative answered the phone, she had no idea why the customer was upset, but by mirroring, "You sound very upset," and using a "tell me more" statement, "What is the problem?" she was able to get the facts of the situation.

Neither Mark nor the customer service representative could begin to solve their respective problems until they had more facts about their situations. Their use of mirroring and "tell me more" helped them get the facts. Notice how few words each one used to get the other person to talk and to provide facts. That is the power of mirroring. When you reflect the other person's feelings with simple "you seem…" or "you sound…" statements, they feel understood, and will start to tell you why they feel that way; that is, they will tell you the facts.

However, neither of these situations will be solved just by mirroring. More communication tools are necessary, tools that will be discussed later. But these two examples show how mirroring helps to peel away layers of feelings about facts and move a discussion down the path to conflict resolution.

EXERCISE: Mirroring Without Words

Directions: In this exercise you will break into pairs and practice **mirroring**, reflecting back the other person's feelings. Take turns speaking and listening. Before you begin write the following words on separate slips of paper or cards: Angry, Happy, Sad, Upset, Frustrated, Glad. Your instructor will give you the rest of the directions.

1. "All right!"
   (Act happy or glad.) _____

2. "This has got to stop!"
   (Act angry or frustrated.) _____

3. "I didn't get the job."
   (Act sad.) _____

4. "I can't take it anymore!"
   (Act angry or upset.) _____

5. "Good morning."
   (Act sad.) _____

6. "I'm fed up."
   (Act frustrated or upset.) _____

7. "Hey you, how's it going?"
   (Act happy or glad.) _____

8. "What's with you?"
   (Act upset or angry.) _____

EXERCISE: Mirroring With Words

Directions: This time use spoken words instead of written words to respond to the following statements. Take turns reading and responding. Use such mirroring phrases as "You look . . ." "You seem . . ." "You sound . . .".

What You Say	**Response**
Example:	
"I can't take all the traffic in this town!"	*"You sound frustrated."*

1. "I'm sick of this!"
(Act upset.)   _____

2. "Oh, it's you."
(Act upset.)   _____

3. "This company drives me crazy!"
(Act frustrated.)   _____

4. "Your department is the worst!"
(Act upset.)   _____

5. "I've had it with you!"
(Act angry.)   _____

6. "I feel like quitting!"
(Act frustrated.)   _____

7. "I can't believe what's happened!"
(Act upset.)   _____

8. "That's it!"
(Sound frustrated.)   _____

HOMEWORK: Practicing Mirroring and Simple Signals

Directions: In this exercise, assume that someone just walked up to you and made the following statements. Respond to each using a simple signal, then respond with mirroring. Write each response on the appropriate line.

Example:
"I've had it with my boss!"

Simple Signal: "What's up?"

Mirroring: "You sound upset."

1. "What is with you?" he yelled.

Simple Signal: _____

Mirroring: _____

2. "Nothing is going right," he said, looking glum.

Simple Signal: _____

Mirroring: _____

3. "Well that's just fine!" she said, as she tossed her pen onto the table.

Simple Signal: _____

Mirroring: _____

4. "What do *you* want?" he snapped.

Simple Signal: _____

Mirroring: _____

5. "Hey, how ya' doing today?" he said with a big smile.

Simple Signal: _____

Mirroring: _____

6. "So who put *you* in charge?" she snarled.

Simple Signal: _____

Mirroring: _____

7. "Great, just great!" and he threw up his hands.

Simple Signal: _____

Mirroring: _____

8. "Good morning! Good morning!" he says, slapping you on the back.

Simple Signal: _____

Mirroring: _____

Name:_____

HOMEWORK: "If I Had a Mirror"

Directions: Look around you for situations where people express only feel-ings (no facts) verbally or non-verbally. It could be someone interacting with you, other people you observe, or even situations from TV or a movie. Briefly describe the situation, including what was said. Tell how you would mirror the person.

Situation   **How I Would Mirror**

Example:
Two people sitting in front of me on
the bus. One said to the other, "My boss
is the worst!"   *"You sound upset."*

1. _____

_____   _____

_____   _____

2. _____

_____   _____

_____   _____

3. _____

_____   _____

_____   _____

Paraphrasing—Understanding Facts Or Feelings

You have learned that mirroring reflects that you understand how someone feels. Another useful listening method called **paraphrasing** lets someone know that you also understand the facts of his message. Paraphrasing simply means saying *in your own words* what you thought you heard. It is an essential listening tool because when you **paraphrase** correctly you send the message that you are listening carefully. Like mirroring, this skill makes people feel not only heard but understood. And more than anything else, people want to be heard and understood.

Don't Be a Parrot

Let's say you own a parrot. We all know that parrots repeat what they hear. So let's say every morning when you get up you grumble, "I hate getting up early." After a few weeks, the parrot repeats, "I hate getting up early." But what if one day the parrot says, "You'd like to sleep in late more often."

You'd probably be astonished because the parrot put what you said into his own words. Parrots aren't capable of that, but humans are—it's called paraphrasing.

As a matter of fact, if you repeat exactly what someone just said, like a parrot, it would probably upset him or her. You'd get a response like, "That's what I just said!" Putting it in your own words means that you've processed and understood a message, not just repeated it without thinking.

Paraphrasing means putting what you heard in your own words, not simply repeating it like a parrot.

Listen For Key Words

Paraphrasing is putting in your own words what you think you heard. To learn to paraphrase, listen for key words. Using key words and re-stating them in your own words helps you paraphrase effectively. Here are a few examples.

Example: "I can't stand it when telemarketers call during dinner!"

Key words	Similar words
can't stand it	frustrating
call during dinner	invade your privacy

Paraphrase: "It's frustrating when telemarketers invade your privacy."

Example: "Local news stations report nothing but violence. You never hear about the positive things people are doing."

Key words	Similar words
nothing but violence	crime
positive things	uplifting stories

Paraphrase: "So you think local news ignores uplifting stories and focuses only on crime."

Example: "I like my job and care about the company, but time with my family comes first."

Key words	Similar words
like my job	enjoy my work
care about the company	devoted
family comes first	top priority is family

Paraphrase: "You enjoy your work and are devoted to your employer, but your family is your top priority."

EXERCISE: Identify the Key Words and Restate Them as a Paraphrase

Directions: Identify key words in the statements below, then use them to paraphrase the statement.

1. I love taking the bus instead of driving my car. I have time to read, and I feel so much less stressed when I get to work.

Key words   **Similar words**

_____   _____

_____   _____

_____   _____

Paraphrase:_____

_____

2. I think the ability to get along with others is one of the key skills people need in the workplace.

Key words   **Similar words**

_____   _____

_____   _____

_____   _____

Paraphrase:_____

_____

3. Medical and dental insurance costs so much now that many people are living without coverage.

Key words   **Similar words**

_____   _____

_____   _____

_____   _____

Paraphrase:_____

_____

4. We may say that education is important, but we spend more on highways than schools.

Key words   **Similar words**

_____   _____

_____   _____

_____   _____

Paraphrase:_____

_____

5. We idolize sports figures and movie stars, but they have faults just like the rest of us.

Key words   **Similar words**

_____   _____

_____   _____

_____   _____

Paraphrase:_____

_____

6. My boss has strict rules and really enforces them. I think that's because he spent fifteen years in the Marines.

Key words   **Similar words**

_____   _____

_____   _____

_____   _____

Paraphrase:_____

_____

7. You can buy groceries, books, even cars off the Internet. I wonder if stores will soon become obsolete.

Key words   **Similar words**

_____   _____

_____   _____

_____   _____

Paraphrase:_____

_____

8. Just because you are out of school does not mean you can stop learning. Today's workplace demands that people keep their skills current.

Key words   **Similar words**

_____   _____

_____   _____

_____   _____

Paraphrase:_____

_____

Paraphrasing Is a Question

When you paraphrase someone's words you're asking a subtle question, "This is what I think you said, am I correct?" Starting a paraphrase with words such as, "So you think…" indicates you are asking if you understand correctly. Here are some other words you can use to start a paraphrase:

"So what I think you're saying is…"

"Let me make sure I understand you…"

"So what I heard you say is…"

"So you think…"

"So you believe…"

Let Them Decide If You Understand

Because paraphrasing is a question, you are looking for the other person to confirm that you understand them. If you paraphrase correctly, you will hear a response like, "Yeah. That's what I'm saying." If you are incorrect, the other person will tell you what you misunderstood. You might hear phrases like:

"No, that's not what I meant. What I said was…"

"Well yeah, that's partially what I said, but I also said…"

"Yeah, pretty much. And I also said…"

Paraphrasing takes concentration on the message. Even if your paraphrase is partially correct, people will be patient with you because it is obvious that you are listening. However, avoid the trap of assuming that you understand. Don't start a paraphrase with, "I understand." If you are wrong it will only upset them. Using some of the starting phrases listed above lets them know you are asking if you understood correctly.

Starting a paraphrase with this is dangerous. Let the other person decide if you understand.

Paraphrase When You Get Facts

Use mirroring only when someone communicates *just feelings* to you. Use paraphrasing when someone communicates facts, or feelings *and* facts. The key point is that when you hear facts—with or without feelings—paraphrase! Let's look at how to paraphrase in both situations: when you get facts, or when you get facts *and* feelings.

What you hear:	What you do:
Feelings only	Mirror
Facts only	Paraphrase
Facts and feelings	Paraphrase

What Are "the Facts?"

When you are actively listening, the facts are the information or opinions stated by the speaker. Some information is factually correct such as, "There are over six billion people on earth." Sometimes people communicate opinions that seem correct to them, but may or may not be true such as, "The world is overpopulated." Either way, to make people feel understood you must paraphrase their "facts" whether they are correct or not. Later we will discuss what to do when their "facts" are wrong. For now, remember this:

When you are listening to others, **the facts = their opinions.**

In other words, to the speaker, what he or she says is the truth. So paraphrase their facts in your own words first. Doing so ensures that you understand the other person's point, and you make him or her feel understood. If you want to argue their facts you can do that later.

Paraphrase When You Hear "Facts Only" Statements

When you hear only facts, you get information or opinions without a lot of emotion. To make sure you understand, paraphrase the facts. Here are some examples of "facts only" statements.

"Facts only" example: "I think we could get more business if we were open more hours."

Paraphrase: "So you think we would attract more customers with extended hours."

"Facts only" example: "I would take the bus to work, but it takes me thirty minutes longer, and I have to transfer three times."

Paraphrase: "You would use public transit if it were faster and more convenient."

New ideas, proposals, or explanations are often "facts only" statements. Misunderstanding such vital information causes confusion and wasted effort in organizations. For that reason paraphrasing "facts only" statements is very important.

Many comments, ideas, and proposals presented at meetings are "facts only" statements. Selectively paraphrasing the input from co-workers makes meetings more productive and, ultimately makes organizations more successful.

EXERCISE: Paraphrasing Facts

Directions: Each of the following is a "facts only" statement and does not contain strong feelings. Using key words, write a paraphrase for each.

Example:

Statement: *"I think the minimum wage should be increased to ten dollars so all working people can make enough money to survive."*

Response: *"You think a higher minimum wage would be fair so all people working could pay their bills."*

1. "I use telephones and computers every day. I couldn't live without them."

Response: _____

_____

2. "We could solve our smog and traffic problems if people used buses more and their cars less."

Response: _____

_____

3. "My new boss speaks three languages and has lived in four countries. She relates well to our ethnically diverse staff."

Response: _____

_____

4. "Our company is so demanding of its employees that I think it should offer three weeks of vacation a year, not just two."

Response: _____

_____

EXERCISE: Paraphrasing Facts Verbally

Directions: Below are statements that are mostly factual. They are meant to be read aloud without too much emotion. Find a partner and take turns reading the statements aloud. Ask your partner to paraphrase what was said.

1. With e-mail, voicemail, pagers, and faxes it is hard to keep up with all of my daily communications.

_____

_____

_____

2. This society is sports crazy. It seems like sports is the only thing people talk about.

_____

_____

_____

3. The 65 mile per hour speed limit isn't dangerous. The real hazards are those drivers talking on the phone, brushing their teeth, or combing their hair.

_____

_____

_____

4. Space exploration is great, but we have more pressing needs like education and the environment.

_____

_____

_____

5. I don't think the media gives you the real story about what is happening in Washington, DC.

_____

_____

_____

6. Ten years ago I had never used a computer; now I couldn't get through the day without one.

_____

_____

_____

Paraphrasing Facts *and* Feelings

Many times the messages we get from people are not only facts, *but also* feelings. We've already discussed the importance of dealing with people's feelings before the facts in order to calm them down. Now we will practice paraphrasing *both* facts and feelings. The key here is to listen for the words that describe feelings, and paraphrase them along with the facts. Let's look at an example.

Luis is upset with Ann because she doesn't fix the copier when she causes a paper jam.

> Luis: "Look Ann, if you jam the copier, fix it or call for service. I'm tired of fixing your problems before I can make my own copies."

> Ann: "So you're frustrated because I keep leaving a mess for you."

> Luis: "Yeah. Stop doing it."

Ann dealt with the feeling (frustration) before she discussed the facts (left a mess). If Ann is going to help Luis calm down, she is correct to start with Luis's feelings first, and then address the facts. Remember, when people are emotional: **Deal with the feelings first, and the facts second.**

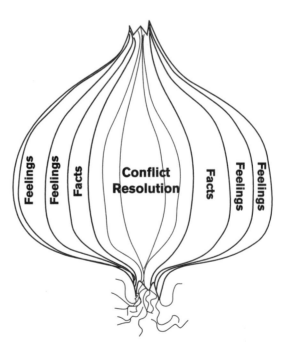

When paraphrasing feelings and facts, peel the onion. Peel away feelings first, then the facts.

EXERCISE: Paraphrasing Facts and Feelings

Directions: Paraphrase these feelings/facts statements. First write down how you would paraphrase the feelings, then write how you would paraphrase the facts.

1. "Bill, I'm upset by the fact that each time it was your turn to drive this month, you've been late, so we've been late to work."

Feelings _____

Facts _____

2. "I've had it! The boss lets everyone but me go to training classes."

Feelings _____

Facts _____

3. "What is with you guys? Every order this week has shipped late, and I'm the one who gets to hear the irate calls from our customers!"

Feelings _____

Facts _____

4. "I've been working here for ten years. I have always been on time and never called in sick, yet I'm still the lowest paid person in the department. This isn't fair!"

Feelings _____

Facts _____

EXERCISE: Paraphrasing Facts and Feelings Verbally

Directions: Below are statements containing both facts and feelings. With a partner take turns reading the statements aloud and paraphrasing each one. Remember to paraphrase feelings first, then facts!

1. (Act angry/frustrated.) I can't stand the way we run meetings around here. They always start late, and never accomplish anything!

_____

_____

_____

2. (Act happy/proud.) I'm terrified of public speaking, but today I gave an excellent presentation at the staff meeting!

_____

_____

_____

3. (Act happy/proud.) Our process improvement team struggled for months, but we eventually came up with ideas that saved the company $500,000!

_____

_____

_____

4. (Act upset/frustrated.) Sam is always late and often leaves early, but the boss never does anything about it!

_____

_____

_____

Do I Paraphrase When Their "Facts" Are Wrong?

Sometimes the "facts" you hear are just plain wrong. Should you paraphrase incorrect information? Although it seems strange, the answer is yes!

But why paraphrase wrong information? Remember, with "active listening" the purpose is to let people know you understand them. They will not be ready to listen to you unless they feel heard, which may even involve paraphrasing incorrect information. Arguing back before they feel heard will not solve anything. Here are two examples.

Troy and Alberto are co-workers. Troy is jealous of Alberto's recent promotion.

> Troy: "I can't believe this!"
> Alberto: "What's the matter?" (*tell me more*) "You sound upset."
>   (*mirrors*)
> Troy: "You got that promotion only because you're a friend of
>   the boss!" (*a fact to Troy*)
> Alberto: "That's not true! I earned it."
> Troy: "No you didn't."
> Alberto: "Yes I did."
> Troy: "No you didn't."

On and on this will go as they both get more upset. Troy is incorrect, but Alberto let himself be drawn into an endless argument by responding to Troy's incorrect fact with, "That's not true!"

Here's a better way for Alberto to handle the situation.

> Troy: "You got that promotion only because you're a friend of
> the boss." (*a fact to Troy*)
> Alberto: "So you think my relationship with the boss deter-
> mined my promotion?" (*paraphrases*)
> Troy: "Yeah."
> Alberto: "What makes you say that?" (*Tell me more, in response to
> an accusation*)
> Troy: "Well, I see you going to lunch with him now and then.
> Nobody else in this department does."
> Alberto: "So you think I got the promotion because I go to lunch
> with the boss occasionally?" (*paraphrases*)
> Troy: "Yeah."

Notice the difference in the second example. It does not spiral into an argument like the first example. Rather than respond with, "That's not true!" Alberto paraphrased Troy's "facts," even though they were probably incorrect. Alberto is much more in control of the conversation. Rather than argue, Alberto asked a question to make Troy state the reasons behind his accusation. Now Alberto has more information when he rebuts Troy's arguments.

Paraphrasing Is Not Agreeing or Apologizing

We may be reluctant to paraphrase someone's "incorrect facts" because the other person might see it as agreement. But Alberto did not say, "I agree with you, Troy. The only reason I got the job is because I'm a friend of the boss." Eventually Alberto will present an opposing point of view, but Troy will not be ready to listen until he feels that Alberto has heard him. That's why it's called active *listening*, not active arguing.

Later in another section you will see how someone in Alberto's position can respond with his own viewpoint. It's called, "Pressing the Talk Button." The key point here is that unless you actively listen to people, they aren't going to listen to you. *So listen first, even if you think they're wrong*, and you'll have your chance to present your viewpoint later.

HOMEWORK: Paraphrase These Feelings and Incorrect Facts

Directions: Below are some statements that contain "facts." Assume the facts are wrong. In the space provided, paraphrase each one without admitting to the incorrect facts. Then write an incorrect response that might escalate the conversation into more intense conflict.

Example: You didn't invite me to that meeting because you are trying to exclude me from the project and take the credit for yourself!

Correct Paraphrase: *So you're upset because you think I'm shutting you out of the project for my personal gain.*

Incorrect Paraphrase: *Oh stop being so paranoid! I just forgot to invite you to the meeting, all right?*

1. This isn't fair! You give all the easy work to Jennifer and Miguel because they try to be your friends, and I get all the lousy projects because I refuse to play office politics.

Correct Paraphrase_____

_____

Incorrect Paraphrase_____

_____

2. Hey, people are telling me you're talking behind my back. Why don't you have some guts and criticize me to my face?

Correct Paraphrase_____

_____

Incorrect Paraphrase_____

_____

3. You knew all day that you had five hot orders, but you waited until five o'clock to dump them on me. Now I have to work late because of you!

Correct Paraphrase_____

_____

Incorrect Paraphrase_____

_____

4. Nobody listens to me around here, and I'm tired of it! Everybody ignores my opinions because of my age. I can see it in their eyes, that look that says, "What does an old guy like him know about these modern issues?"

Correct Paraphrase_____

_____

Incorrect Paraphrase_____

_____

"Pressing the Talk Button"
—Presenting Your Views

"So," you might be thinking, "I see why active listening is important, but don't I get to tell my side?" Of course you do. Effective communication means that all people involved are able to present their views and feel that their views are heard. So it is very important that you present your viewpoint. But it is one thing to just start talking; it is another to be understood.

If you want to be understood, others must be ready to listen to you. People are much more open to considering other viewpoints if they first feel understood. So like it or not, **if you want to be understood, you must help the other person feel understood first**. That is why we introduced listening skills first. Now, here are the methods for making sure you get to present your views. This section is called **"Pressing the Talk Button."** Here's why.

Picture yourself using a walkie-talkie. When you listen, you hold it up to your ear. When you talk, you press the button on the side and speak into the microphone.

The listening skills you've learned so far—simple signals, mirroring and paraphrasing—are like using a walkie-talkie. You listen first to make sure you understand the message. Yes, you do talk as well, but you are primarily responding to indicate that you understand the message such as, "You look upset," or "So you're frustrated because I forgot to call." What you haven't done yet, however, is to present your side of the story.

When you present your viewpoint you are "pressing the talk button"—communicating your opinions. But it won't matter what you say if the other person is not listening on his or her "walkie-talkie." In this section you will learn how to make sure someone is ready to hear you before you speak. Here is how it works.

Pressing the talk button involves four steps:

1. Calm the person by using active listening techniques.

2. Use a short "understanding statement."

3. Ask if you can present your side.

4. If no, go back to step one. If yes, present your views.

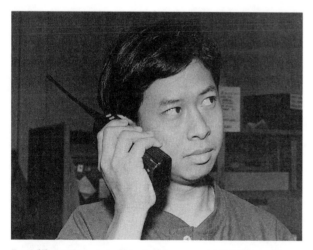

Just like using a walkie-talkie, you can't talk and listen at the same time.

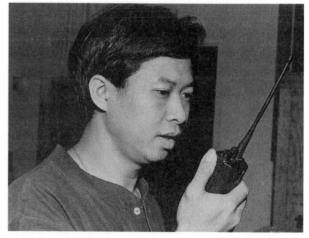

Make sure the other person is ready to listen before you "press the talk button."

Step ❶   Help the Person Calm Down.

The best way to calm people down is to listen to them. You know how to do that—use active listening. Keep in mind that you must deal with a person's feelings (usually anger or frustration) before you talk about facts.

"Yes" Is a Sign They Feel Heard

A good sign that you have listened adequately is when you hear "Yes," or "Yes, that's right." When someone says "Yes," what they are really saying is, *"Yes, you heard everything I said and I feel understood."* When you have listened and reached a "Yes" statement, there is much less tension. Now that person will be better able to listen to your point of view. Anything other than a simple "Yes" is a sign that you must keep listening.

Signs They Feel Heard

"Yeah, that's right."
"Uh huh, you got it."
"Yes. That's what I'm saying."

Signs They Do Not Feel Completely Heard

"No, that's not what I'm saying."
"Well yes, but there's also…"
"Yes, and I also think…"

Whenever you get anything other than an unqualified yes, keep listening. Use paraphrasing to understand any additional points.

When you hear this word in response to your active listening, you know the other person feels understood.

Step ② Use a Short "Understanding Statement."

Once you hear some type of "Yes" response, and the person seems to feel understood, use a short statement to indicate that you see their point of view and understand the feelings. It doesn't mean you agree (although that's okay too!); it just means you understand. Here are some examples:

"I see what you mean."
"I can understand what you're saying."
"I can see the problem."
"I understand why you feel that way."

It's important to use these statements genuinely, and not too quickly. (How can you understand someone's point of view if he hasn't had a chance to express it?) If you are less than genuine, or you use this step too soon, you will only cause more anger. If you think you won't sound genuine using an understanding statement, don't use it. It's better to skip this step than to sound insincere.

EXERCISE: More Understanding Statements

Directions: Think of other understanding statements you could use.

Example: "I see what you mean."

1. _____

2. _____

3. _____

Step ③ Ask If You Can Press the Talk Button

Before presenting your point of view it helps to ask other people if they'd like to hear it. Then they can get ready to hear your side, and they are commiting to listening. Use phrases like these to **press the talk button**:

"Can I tell you my views?"

"May I explain my situation?"

"How about if I explain myself?"

"May I tell you how I see the situation?"

If people say no, then they aren't ready to listen, so go back to step one—active listening—and find out what else they have to say.

EXERCISE: Asking to Press the Talk Button

Directions: What are some other ways to ask someone if you can press the talk button?

Example:
"May I tell you how I see things?"

1. _____

2. _____

3. _____

Step ④ Present Your Point of View

Now you explain your point of view. Remember to present facts, and don't blame.

> Tim: "Why did you choose Tony for the project? I was the most qualified!"
>
> Joe: "So you're really upset with my decision." *(Paraphrases)*
>
> Tim: "You bet I am! I have over five years of experience, but Tony's only been on the job six months!"
>
> Joe: "So you're upset because you think I overlooked you, the more qualified person." *(Paraphrases)*
>
> Tim: "Yes." (A bit calmer now)
>
> Joe: "I can see why you'd be upset. May I explain why I made the decision I did?" *(Understanding statement and asks to push the talk button)*
>
> Tim: "Yeah, I guess."
>
> Joe: "You are the most experienced, but I wanted to give one of the younger employees a chance to work on a project."

Joe paraphrased Tim, making sure Tim felt understood. He made a brief understanding statement and asked to push the talk button before he explained himself. Tim may not like Joe's answers, but at least Joe listened to his concerns and made sure Tim was ready to listen before he explained himself.

When Joe said, "I can see why you're upset," he wasn't agreeing that he'd made a bad decision. He was saying, "I've listened to you to understand why you are mad." When Joe said he understood, it was more genuine because he had paraphrased Tim twice already, which helped Tim calm down enough to listen.

If you say something that upsets your listener, go back to step one. Listen actively because he is still upset and has stopped listening.

Pressing the Talk Button too Early

We often present our point of view before the other person is ready to listen. Here is an example of pressing the talk button too early.

Miguel: "I have had it!"

Stephanie: "Wow, you're upset." (*Active listening – mirroring*)

Miguel: "Of course I'm upset. You borrowed my tools and I didn't have them for an important job!"

Stephanie: "It's not my fault. Somebody stole my tools."

Miguel: "I don't care that you lost your stupid tools. I needed mine and I didn't have them. Now the boss is mad at me because an order for an important customer was late. All because of you!"

What did Stephanie do wrong here? If you say she pressed the talk button too soon, you are right. She listened for a moment, then began to defend herself. Miguel did not have a chance to express all of his frustrations before Stephanie spoke, so he came back with anger. Stephanie couldn't change the fact that Miguel didn't have his tools, but she could have listened more and helped Miguel feel understood before she pressed the talk button.

Here is another example of how *not* to press the talk button.

> Matt: "Why did you hire Judy as the new supervisor without advertising the position? That's not fair. I didn't even get a chance to interview for the job."
>
> Ron: "I know how you feel, but my decision is final."
> *(Understanding statement, pressed the talk button)*
>
> Matt: "What do you mean you know how I feel? You aren't the one who was cheated out of a promotion! Your decision may be final, but it wasn't fair!"

What did Ron do wrong? First, he didn't paraphrase Matt and give him a chance to vent his anger completely. His second mistake was saying, "I know how you feel," too cooly and quickly. Next, he pushed the talk button without checking with Matt; then he answered abruptly with an attitude of, "That's just the way it is." No wonder Matt was furious.

HOMEWORK: Pressing the Talk Button

Directions: In each of the situations below identify what Speaker 2 did wrong in regard to the four steps required to press the talk button. The four steps are: listen actively; state that you understand; ask to push the talk button; talk, but don't blame.

SITUATION  1

Speaker 1: "I can't stand this!"

Speaker 2: "What's wrong?"

Speaker 1: "You've given me all the weekend shifts! I'm the only one who works every weekend!"

Speaker 2: "Too bad. Five people are on vacation."

What did Speaker 2 do wrong? _____

SITUATION 2

Speaker 1: "Where have you been?"

Speaker 2: "Wow, you're upset."

Speaker 1: "Of course I'm upset. It's eight o'clock! You were supposed to be home at six!"

Speaker 2: "So you're angry because I'm two hours late."

Speaker 1: "Yes! Two hours!"

Speaker 2: "I can see why you'd feel that way. May I explain why?"

Speaker 1: "All right, but make it good."

Speaker 2: "I tried to call at six and seven but you were blabbing away on the phone as usual and I couldn't get through."

What did Speaker 2 do wrong? _____

SITUATION 3

Speaker 1: "There you are!"

Speaker 2: "You look angry."

Speaker 1: "Of course I am. Three weeks I've waited for you to pay me back and you haven't given me a dime!"

Speaker 2: "I understand."

Speaker 1: "What do you mean you understand? Where's my money?"

What did Speaker 2 do wrong? _____

_____

SITUATION 4

Speaker 1: "Great job! Thanks to you, I went to the eleven o'clock meeting with no report! I looked like a fool in front of my boss!"

Speaker 2: "Let me explain."

Speaker 1: "No, you let me explain how my boss yelled at me in front of the entire staff for being unprepared and disorganized! Thanks for all your help!"

Speaker 2: "I can explain this."

Speaker 1: "Explain? Explain what? That my boss thinks I'm an idiot thanks to you? Forget your explanations. I've had it with you!"

What did Speaker 2 do wrong? _____

_____

When Others Won't Cooperate

Despite your efforts to communicate effectively and respectfully, some people may still be unwilling to cooperate. This section provides some helpful tips for dealing with uncooperative, aggressive, or rude behavior. These tips will help you stay calm and focused despite continued resistance. To stay calm and in control, again use the active listening tools.

Following is an example of someone who is uncooperative, even rude, despite your best efforts to communicate respectfully. Suppose you have a co-worker, Brent, who interrupts you frequently at meetings, which bothers you. You approach Brent using the five steps for starting difficult conversations. The conversation goes as follows:

"Hey Brent, you got a minute?" (*check the timing*)

"Sure."

"In staff meetings the last few weeks you've interrupted me while I was speaking. (*facts*) That frustrates me because I'm not able to get my points out completely. (*feelings*) I'd appreciate it if you'd let me finish when I'm speaking in meetings. (*needs*) Okay?" (*ask for response*)

"Oh stop being so sensitive."

"What?"

"You heard me. Stop being so sensitive. Those meetings are chances to debate ideas, and sometimes they get brutal. If I feel the need to interrupt you to make my point, I will. You're really fragile!"

What do you do now? How do you respond to such a rude reply?

Respond with Active Listening

What you must **not** do is respond with a similar attitude. Here are some responses that will not work if you want to resolve this situation positively.

> "All right fine, Brent. If you're going to be a jerk, I can be one too."

> "What a jerk! I can see why no one likes working with you."

These or similar responses will add to the conflict. In addition, you will have come down to Brent's level. Now you're just as rude and inconsiderate as he is!

To stay in control and keep the conversation positive use active listening tools to respond to Brent. Consider Brent's responses:

"Stop being so sensitive."
"These meetings are chances for give and take."
"You're really fragile!"

These are "facts only" statements. Remember from active listening that all of our communication fits into two categories: facts or feelings. When you get facts, paraphrase. So a great way to counter Brent calmly is to paraphrase his statements, no matter how rude they are. Here's how:

Brent says	You respond
"Stop being so sensitive."	"So you think I'm overly sensitive because I asked you to stop interrupting me?"
"These meetings can be brutal give and take sessions."	"So you think any behavior is justified in our staff meetings, and I should accept any interruptions?"
"You're really fragile."	"So you think I'm weak because I asked you to stop interrupting me?"

Paraphrasing uncooperative statements like Brent's keeps you from responding with anger. Also, you show the faults in Brent's views.

Here is a list of other typical uncooperative "facts only" statements someone like Brent might use, and words to paraphrase them.

Uncooperative statement	Paraphrase response
"Don't tell me what to do."	"So you think that asking you to stop interrupting is telling you what to do?"
"Who made you my boss?"	"So you think I'm trying to be the boss by asking you to stop interrupting me?"
"It's a tough world. Just grow up."	"So you think I'm being childish by asking you to stop interrupting me?"
"Shut up."	"So you're telling me to stop asking you not to interrupt me?"

Notice in each of the responses that you are not responding with a rude
reply. You are calmly paraphrasing uncooperative remarks. In doing so,
you are exposing how unreasonable they are. And since you are asking a
question, you are asking Brent, or anyone else, to agree that they are being
uncooperative, or worse.

Also notice that each time the paraphrase response to Brent's comments
includes the original request, "So when I ask you to stop interrupting me
you think…" you are restating your point, and—assuming it is a reasonable request—it further highlights Brent's uncooperative attitude.

Be careful. This approach will backfire if you paraphrase sarcastically.
When paraphrasing an uncooperative statement, keep your tone of voice
calm and non-judgmental.

Exercise: Paraphrasing Uncooperative Statements

Directions: Below are more uncooperative phrases that Brent could have used in this situation. Each one is a "facts only" statement, so respond by paraphrasing. Include in your paraphrase the original request, which was that Brent stop interrupting you.

Example:

Brent says, "Hey, it's not just me. Everyone interrupts everyone else in that meeting."

Your paraphrase: "So you think I'm picking on you by asking you to stop interrupting me?"

Brent says:

1. "Um, excuse me, but when did you become my manager?"

Your paraphrase: _____

_____

2. "Oh please. Worry about something important."

Your paraphrase: _____

_____

3. "I can't be bothered with your little sensitivities."

Your paraphrase: _____

_____

4. "Get a thicker skin, will you?"

Your paraphrase: _____

_____

In some cases, people like Brent might back down after your paraphrase. They may see how uncooperative they are and agree to meet your request. The conversation might go something like this.

Brent: "Oh stop being so sensitive!"

You: "So you think I'm overly sensitive because I'm asking you to stop interrupting me?"

Brent: "Yes. I mean, no. I don't know. I guess not. I mean, I know I shouldn't interrupt you, but I want to express my ideas when I think of them. If I wait until you are finished, I might forget them."

So now Brent has agreed that interrupting you is not necessarily the right thing to do. But he also told you he wants to be able to state his ideas quickly. To work out a mutually-agreeable situation, now you focus on how you can both get your needs met. Perhaps you work it out that Brent at least raises his hand to let you know he has an idea. Now that Brent seems more open, it is up to you to find solutions that work for you *and* him. This is "win-win" negotiating.

While you have not solved the problem yet, your ability to stay calm and paraphrase Brent's initial uncooperative statements has led you to a point of potential resolution.

If at First You Don't Succeed...
Restate Your Request and Ask for Cooperation

Some people don't turn cooperative quite so fast. For whatever reason, they respond to your paraphrase with further resistance. In that case, you can acknowledge their viewpoint, however rude it may be, then restate your need, and ask again for cooperation. Here are the steps:

1. Acknowledge their viewpoint.
2. Restate your need.
3. Ask to work it out.

For example, you ask Brent to stop interrupting, but he responds...

> "Oh stop being so sensitive!"
>
> "So you think I'm being overly sensitive because I'm asking you to stop interrupting me?"
>
> "Yeah."

You respond with...

> "Well, you may feel that way, but I still don't want to be interrupted. So how can we work this out?"

There are three parts to your last response:

1. Acknowledged his point: "Well, you may feel the way."
2. Restated your need: "But I still don't want to be interrupted."
3. Asked to work it out: "So how can we work this out?"

This type of response maintains your control because you are still not responding emotionally to Brent's lack of cooperation. You do not deny his viewpoint, but by repeating your need, you send a strong message, "I'm not backing down." Finally by saying, "How can we work this out?" you are saying to Brent, "Despite all of your resistance I'm willing to find a solution. Are you?"

"How can we work this out?" is an open-ended question. It cannot be answered with a yes or no, which is powerful because it makes Brent either come up with solutions, or say, "I don't want to work this out."

Exercise: Don't Give In

Directions: Each of the following exercises creates a situation where you have repeatedly tried to get someone to cooperate with you, but he or she refuses. For each one acknowledge the other's position, repeat your needs, and request to work out the situation.

Example: You ask a co-worker to stop using your computer at lunch to surf the Web because he interrupts the programs you are running.

He responds: "Look, the computer is company property, not your property."
Your response: "So you won't stop using the machine during lunch because you think my computer is public property for all employees?"
He responds: "Yeah."

Acknowledge: "Well I'm sorry you feel that way."
Your need: "But I still need my programs to be uninterrupted when they're running."
Ask to work it out: "So how can we work this out?"

1. You ask a co-worker to stop listening in and commenting on your personal phone calls.

She responds: "Oh relax, we're like family here. There are no secrets among us."
You paraphrase: "So you're saying you believe we all have a right to listen to each other's phone calls?"
Her response: "Yeah."

Acknowledge: _____

Restate your need: _____

Ask to work it out: _____

2. A co-worker has been ordering you around, even though he is not your boss. You ask him to stop, and you say that you prefer to take direction only from your boss.

He responds: "Look, I've been here a lot longer than you, and if I see something you're supposed to do, I'll tell you."

Your paraphrase: "So even though I prefer to take directions only from my boss, you'll continue to give me orders because you have seniority?"

His response: "Yeah."

Acknowledge: _____

Restate your need: _____

Ask to work it out: _____

3. You work a swing (evening) shift, and share a workspace with a co-worker on the day shift. When you arrive the work area is extremely messy, and it takes you a long time to clean it up. You have asked your co-worker to do some basic cleanup and organizing by putting away the tools and picking up the scrap parts left around the area.

She responds: "Look. You're a neat freak. You want everything perfectly in its place. I don't have time for that. Deal with a little mess."

You paraphrase: "So you think I'm overly concerned about neatness by asking you to put away the tools and clean up the scrap parts?"

Her response: "Yeah."

Acknowledge: _____

Restate your need: _____

Ask to work it out:_____

What If They <u>Still</u> Will Not Cooperate?

Even the steps described here may not be enough to get someone to cooperate. He or she may respond to your last question, "How can we work this out?" with a response like, "We can't."

At this point you have some decisions to make. You can accept the situation and respond with something like the following.

> "Well I'm sorry you feel that way. I was hoping we could work this out."

Sometimes people have political power in an organization, and you are forced to accept the situation. At the very least you have solicited cooperation in a respectful yet assertive manner, and you have not gotten yourself into trouble by responding with anger or pettiness.

Or you can let the other person know that you might seek other recourse, such as taking the issue to higher management. In that case, you would respond with something like the following.

> "Well I'm sorry you feel that way, but I still don't want to be interrupted. So I guess that I am going to have to take up the matter with the boss."

Before saying something like this, be sure you are ready to carry out what you say. Ask yourself how receptive your manager would be. If you choose to pursue the issue, the assertive yet respectful way you have handled the situation so far will help your case. The other person cannot point to any rudeness or lack of cooperation on your part. Workplace politics is not easy, but by using your communication skills wisely you increase the chances of making your case successfully.

Listening Blockers

Now that you've been introduced to the tools of good listening, let's look at some negative behaviors that get in the way. We call them **listening blockers**.

Football blockers prevent defensive players from getting to the ball carrier. Listening blockers prevent us from hearing what others say.

On a football team, blockers stop defensive players from getting to the ball carrier. In everyday life, blockers stop us from listening effectively and thus communicating well.

Below are descriptions of listening blockers. Which roles do you play and which ones do you recognize in others?

Listening Blockers—Which Pattern Describes You?

The Daydreamer

The daydreamer looks like she's listening, but she's actually imagining what she would buy if she won the lottery. She may sound like she's listening because she says, "Uh-huh, I see, sure ..." at the right times. She "channel surfs" in her mind until she finds an interesting topic, then she drifts away. Unfortunately, she misses lots of important information. In addition, the speaker can see that far-off look in the daydreamer's eyes.

Example:

> Eduardo: "So my boss said last month I'd get a raise soon."
>
> Melissa: "Uh-huh." (Thinking about her plans for tonight.)
>
> Eduardo: "But I haven't seen one yet. Do you think I should confront him or quit?"
>
> Melissa: (After a pause when she realizes Eduardo asked her a question.) "Yeah, definitely."
>
> Eduardo: "Yeah to which one?"
>
> Melissa: "I'm sorry, what was the question again?"
>
> Eduardo: "Forget it. You weren't even listening!" (Walks away angry)

Do you ever daydream in a conversation? _____

Why? _____

Do you know someone else who does? _____

The Identifier

"I can identify with that." Everything the identifier hears reminds him of something similar that happened to him. You try to tell him about a problem with your boss, and he interrupts you with a story about his lousy boss. He plays "one-upmanship" by relating a similar incident, one just a little bigger and better than yours. The identifier is boring, because he never lets you talk about yourself.

Example:

Chuck: "So I came out of the theater and I realized I had left my wallet inside!"

Tanya: "That happened to me once on a bus."

Chuck: "I went back inside, and it was gone. I don't know what I'm going to do."

Tanya: "I chased the bus to the next stop and finally got it. But I had to run six blocks!"

Chuck: "What are you talking about? Don't you care about my situation?"

Do you ever play the Identifier in a conversation? _____

Why?_____

Do you know someone else who does? _____

The Consultant

In real life, a consultant is hired to give advice. But the consultant as a listening blocker is one who gives advice or solves your problem without being asked. The consultant is so busy finding the perfect solution that she doesn't hear the real problem. Instead of listening, she is rehearsing her response. Because she doesn't listen to the whole story, she ends up giving advice that doesn't work.

Example:

> Sam: "I have to be downtown tomorrow night for a party, but my car broke down."
>
> Ann: "Oh? Your car broke down?" (At this point, Ann tunes out to find a solution for the car. But Sam keeps talking.)
>
> Sam: "So my friend said she'd lend me her car. Now I have to decide what to wear. It's supposed to be fancy. Got any ideas?"
>
> Ann: "Maybe you could take the train instead."
>
> Sam: "Huh?"

Have you ever played the role of the Consultant? _____

Why? _____

Do you know someone else who does? _____

The Derailer

Picture a train speeding down the tracks. Imagine that someone rolls a boulder into its path; the train derails. Now, imagine a conversation in which the speaker presents a train of thought for consideration. The listener doesn't like it, so he derails it! He changes the subject so fast and so well that the speaker doesn't even know what happened. The train of conversation stops. Sometimes, the derailer tells a joke to stop serious conversation. And whatever the speaker was discussing is forgotten.

Example:

Erin: "Nick, I need to talk with you."

Nick: "What's up?"

Erin: "You opened my mail yesterday, and I'm upset about it."

Nick: "Wait a minute. You owe me twenty dollars. This is the third time you haven't paid me back!"

Have you ever played the Derailer? _____

Why? _____

Do you know someone else who does? _____

The Interrupter

The interrupter is the most obvious of all the blockers. She just never lets anyone finish!

Example:

Chau: "Mary, do you have a minute?"

Mary: "Sure, Chau."

Chau: "I need to talk to you about this phone bill."

Mary: "I know what you're going to say. I talk on the phone too long."

Chau: "Well, actually …"

Mary: "But most of those calls aren't mine."

Chau: "What I'm trying to say is …"

Mary: "Let's call the phone company. I think they messed up."

Chau: (Angry) "Mary, let me finish speaking!"

Have you ever been an Interrupter? _____

Why? _____

Do you know someone else who is? _____

EXERCISE: Identifying the Listening Blocker

Directions: Sit with a partner and take turns being the speaker and the listening blocker. The speaker must figure out what listening blocker is used. Brief topics are provided for the speaker. Guidelines are provided for the listening blocker that describe which type of blocker you are. (The listening blocker can look at the information provided to the speaker, but the speaker cannot look at the guidelines for the blocker.)

Speaker
Start talking about where you were born. Describe the country, state, or city.

Listening Blocker
Be an interrupter. Ask questions, but don't listen to the answers. Shortly after your partner starts speaking, ask a question. Don't let him or her fully answer before you ask another question. Say things like, "Oh really? Did you live there long? Did you like it? Isn't it amazing all the different places people are from?" Don't give him or her much of a chance to speak.

Speaker
Start telling the listener how you get to school—car, bus, walk, etc. Then describe how long it takes you, your route, etc.

Listening Blocker
Be an identifier. Listen and then say that you get to school the same way, then start telling about your experiences. For instance, "I drive my car too. I think it's a hassle. I don't like parking it in the lot, because I'm afraid someone will scratch it. And I've gotten five parking tickets this year. "

Speaker

Start talking about problems you are having with your car. You could describe how you often have trouble starting it and the brakes are wearing out. You have been procrastinating about taking it to a mechanic because it will probably cost a lot.

Listening Blocker

Be a consultant. Listen to your partner's car problems, and make suggestions to solve them like, "You should go to my mechanic. She's great." Or, "Maybe you should get a new car. How about a Honda?"

Speaker

Start telling the listener that you like this class. You're learning practical communication skills that will help you at work and at home, and you think more people should take this class.

Listening Blocker

Be a daydreamer. Let the person talk. When he or she finishes say, "What was that?"

HOMEWORK: Identifying Other Blockers

Directions: Observe people who are using listening blockers. On the lines below write their names, the blockers they used, and what behaviors you saw.

Person   Blocker / Behavior Used

Example:
  My friend, Ed.   *Interrupter / Never lets me finish!*

1. _____   _____

2. _____   _____

3. _____   _____

How to Deal with a Poor Listener

To this point you have looked mostly at your own listening blocks. But how do you deal with someone else who is a poor listener? You already know! **Use these three steps from the chapter on Starting Difficult Conversations:**

1. **State the facts.**

2. **State your feelings.**

3. **State your needs.**

When someone is doing a poor job of listening, let's say interrupting you, state the facts of the situation.

"Craig, you've interrupted me three times." (*facts*)

"I feel frustrated by that." (*feelings*)

"I need you to let me finish speaking." (*needs*)

This works for any poor listening habit. Just remember–state the facts by describing the behavior!

Poor listeners are very frustrating! But there are ways to deal with them: use facts, feelings, needs.

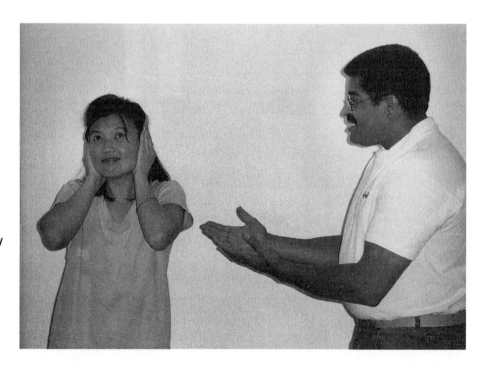

EXERCISE: Dealing With a Poor Listener

Directions: Below are the previous examples of listening blockers. In each one suppose that you are the one dealing with the listening blocker. On the lines provided, write in the kind of blocker you're dealing with, and how you would confront the blocker using facts, feelings and needs.

SITUATION 1

Eduardo: "So my boss said last month I'd get a raise soon."
Melissa: "Uh-huh." (Thinking about her plans for tonight.)
Eduardo: "But I haven't seen one yet. Do you think I should confront him or quit?"
Melissa: (After a pause when she realizes Eduardo asked her a question.) "Yeah, definitely."
Eduardo: "Yeah to which one?"
Melissa: "I'm sorry, what was the question again?"

Listening Blocker: _____

You are Eduardo. How would you deal with Melissa? _____

_____

_____

SITUATION 2

Chuck: "So I came out of the theater and I realized I had left my wallet inside!"
Tanya: "That happened to me once on a bus."
Chuck: "I went back inside, and it was gone. I don't know what I'm going to do."
Tanya: "I chased the bus to the next stop and finally got it. But I had to run six blocks!"

Listening Blocker: _____

You are Chuck. How would you deal with Tanya?_____

_____

_____

SITUATION ❸

Sam: "I have to be downtown tomorrow night for a party, but my car broke down."

Ann: "Oh? Your car broke down?" (At this point, Ann tunes out to find a solution for the car. But Sam keeps talking.)

Sam: "So my friend said she'd lend me her car. Now I have to decide what to wear. It's supposed to be fancy. Got any ideas?"

Ann: "Maybe you could take the train instead."

Listening Blocker: _____

You are Sam. How do you deal with Ann? _____

_____

_____

SITUATION ❹

Chau: "Mary, do you have a minute?"

Mary: "Sure, Chau."

Chau: "I need to talk to you about this phone bill."

Mary: "I know what you're going to say. I talk on the phone too long."

Chau: "Well, actually ..."

Mary: "But most of those calls aren't mine."

Chau: "What I'm trying to say is ..."

Mary: "Let's call the phone company. I think they messed up."

Listening Blocker: _____

You are Chau. How do you deal with Mary? _____

_____

_____

HOMEWORK: Dealing With Poor Listeners

Directions: Below are three situations in which you must deal with a poor listener. Beneath the descriptions write down what you would say to respond to the poor listening behavior. Include facts, feelings, and needs in your answer.

1. Dave the Derailer

Your friend, Dave, borrows your truck on weekends to do chores around his house. Twice he has brought the truck back dirty and with an empty gas tank. You started to talk to him about it and twice he has derailed the conversation onto other topics. Address his derailing behavior.

_____

_____

_____

2. Chris the Consultant

You've been having trouble with your boss. You talk over your problems with your co-worker, Chris, who is a "consultant" listening blocker. Three times you've stopped by Chris' desk to vent your frustrations and immediately he's telling you what you should do to solve the problem. You like Chris and want a friend in the office you can talk to, but you don't always want advice. Address Chris' consulting behavior.

_____

_____

_____

3. Ian the Interrupter

Your friend, Ian, is an excellent interrupter. Nobody interrupts people better than Ian. You can't remember a time he hasn't interrupted you at least once in a conversation. You and Ian are trying to decide what to do for fun this evening, but he's interrupted you three times already. Address Ian's interrupting behavior.

_____

_____

_____

Using Active Listening to Understand Directions

As mentioned in the introduction to this book, one reason people get fired is that they cannot follow directions. Paraphrasing and asking questions are excellent techniques for clarifying instructions, and in this section you will learn how to apply them.

Most workplaces are extremely busy. Phones are ringing, customers want service, pagers are beeping and co-workers are talking. In this setting it is easy to misunderstand someone's directions. In addition, your boss is very busy and doesn't have a lot of time to spend with you. When your boss asks you to do something, directions are hasty, as few bosses have time to write things down. In this kind of chaotic setting misunderstandings happen regularly.

In a job, it's very important to make sure you understand directions. Active listening can help avoid misunderstandings.

Misunderstandings Hurt You!
Have you ever heard these comments?

"Why did you do it that way?"

"That's not what I wanted!"

"That's not what I asked you to do!"

"Who asked you to do that? Not me!"

These sorts of misunderstandings are always frustrating and often painful. They usually mean repeating work, thus frustrating you, your boss, and your customers. At worst, you could be blamed for the misunderstanding—even if it wasn't your fault because you received unclear directions. **To avoid these situations, ask questions and paraphrase.** Asking questions clarifies details, and paraphrasing makes sure you understand the directions clearly. Paraphrasing is especially helpful if you get confusing or unorganized information.

Here are two examples:

> Boss: "Hey Mike, I've got to go to a meeting. While I'm gone
> will you clean up the place?"
>
> Mike: "Sure."

Later ...

> Boss: "Mike, what happened? I asked you to clean up the place!
> These windows are still dirty!"
>
> Mike: "I cleaned the tables and floor. I didn't know you wanted
> me to do the windows too."
>
> Boss: "What do you think clean up the place means? Can't you
> follow directions?"

Make Sure You Understand

This situation happened because Mike's boss was not specific in his directions, and Mike didn't clarify what was meant by "clean up the place." Here is the same situation with questions and paraphrasing.

> Mike: "Hey boss, can you tell me what things you want
> cleaned? Walls, counters, ovens?"
>
> Boss: "Counters, tables, and windows."
>
> Mike: "Okay."

In this example, Mike asked a question to pull out the details of what his boss meant by "clean up the place." This time he heard about the windows. Mike could have pulled out the details with paraphrasing as well. He could have said something like this:

> Mike: "So, when you say clean up the place, do you mean floors
> and tables?"
>
> Boss: "Yes, but also do the windows."
>
> Mike: "Got it."

EXERCISE: Be Like Mike

Directions: What are three other ways—either with a direct question or a paraphrase—that Mike could have clarified his boss's directions?

1. _____

2. _____

3. _____

Don't Just Say, "Okay"

Often it's easier to just say, "Okay" to the boss when we get directions. We don't want to look stupid or uncooperative, or to seem like we are questioning authority. But misunderstanding directions has serious negative consequences. So the challenge is to clarify instructions quickly and confidently. Here are some helpful quick starter words.

Paraphrasing: When you want to make sure you understand the details.

> "Let me make sure I've got this ..."
>
> "So to quickly review what you're asking ..."
>
> "May I just quickly clarify? You want ..."
>
> "So you want me to ..."
>
> "Let me just make sure I heard you correctly ..."

Asking Questions: When you need more information.

> "Anything specific you want me to cover?"
>
> "Can you tell me what _____ means, exactly?"
>
> "Can you quickly list the items you want me to do?"
>
> "What would that entail?"
>
> "What are some of the things you want me to cover?"

EXERCISE: Following Each Other's Instructions

Directions: Pair up with a partner. Take turns reading to each other the following directions. Some directions are vague and you must ask for details. Others are detailed and you'll want to paraphrase.

1. "Will you close up the store tonight?"

_____

_____

2. "Take care of things while I'm on vacation, okay?"

_____

_____

3. "While I'm gone please do the laundry. Remember never to mix white and colored clothes. Don't wash anything in hot water. And don't put cotton things in the dryer.

_____

_____

4. "This report is too hard to read. I want wider columns, a larger font size, and totals at the bottom of each page. Are these numbers approved by the accounting department?"

_____

_____

5. "I want this party for Ed to be the best going-away party we've ever held."

_____

_____

6. "I need twenty half-inch steel pipes cut into two foot lengths. Make sure there are no sharp edges on the ends. And package them in bundles of four. Oh, and make sure you use sturdy boxes this time!"

_____

_____

Name:_____

HOMEWORK: Clarifying Instructions

Directions: Below are brief statements of instructions you might get at work. Some can be clarified with a question, while others are best clarified by paraphrasing. Read each statement, then choose the best way to clarify the instructions.

Example:	**Response:**
"See that this report is perfect, Okay?"	*"What would perfect look like to you?"*

1. "I'm leaving early. Make sure the lobby is clean, the lights are turned off, the front door is locked, and the security system is turned on."

   _____

   _____

2. "Take care of everything in the shop tomorrow, okay?"

   _____

3. "It's your job to see that we hit the production goal this week."

   _____

4. "These two printers must be sent to our Florida office, overnight FedEx. But before you do that, repair their power cords. And when you are fixing the cords, please put in new printer rollers."

   _____

   _____

5. "Make sure the new employees starting this week feel welcomed."

   _____

Handling Insults:
Baseballs or Bullets

You've just learned some valuable active listening skills. But what happens when you use good listening skills and someone doesn't play fair, and insults you? In this section you will learn to handle insulting behavior and still remain calm.

Picture a baseball catcher who wears a lot of protective equipment: a mask, a chest protector, and shin guards. When a pitched ball hits the equipment, the ball bounces off, and the catcher is safe. Would the catcher's equipment stop a bullet? No, of course not. The catcher would be seriously hurt.

Insults and offensive remarks are like **baseballs** and **bullets**. Some remarks bounce off harmlessly (baseballs), and some seriously hurt (bullets). Like the catcher, each of us wears our own protective equipment. Some wear heavy duty equipment and are not easily hurt. Others wear lighter equipment and are injured easily. There is no right amount of protection. Each person is different, so we must judge for ourselves what insults us and what does not.

A baseball wouldn't hurt this catcher if it hit him, but a bullet would. Verbal baseballs are comments that bounce off of us, while bullets are comments that hurt or offend us. Each of us is different in deciding what comments offend, and what comments bounce off.

EXERCISE: Identifying Baseballs and Bullets

Directions: In this section mildly insulting remarks are baseballs and more insulting remarks are bullets. What is a baseball to one person may be a bullet to another. Following are some examples. Make a check in the appropriate box if you consider these terms to be baseballs or bullets.

Someone calls you ...	Baseball	Bullet
1. a loser	_____	_____
2. a dummy	_____	_____
3. a goofball	_____	_____
4. a racist term	_____	_____
5. a complete idiot	_____	_____
6. a nerd	_____	_____
7. messy	_____	_____
8. forgetful	_____	_____
9. irresponsible	_____	_____
10. dangerous	_____	_____
11. ugly	_____	_____

You may have said, "It depends," as you went through the list. It depends on who said it or how and where it was said. Want to know how to deal with both baseballs and bullets? The next section provides some useful insights.

Dealing with Minor Insults (Baseballs)

Asking Questions

A baseball is a mildly insulting remark. A good way to handle baseballs is to ask questions. You keep from getting angry and you don't get pulled into an ugly conversation. Following are two examples. Mike and Bill worked on a project together and just got the report back.

Mike: "Here's your report. You made a few stupid mistakes."

Bill: "Hey! Don't call me stupid! You're stupid!"

In this example Bill reacts immediately to the word "stupid." He gets defensive and insults Mike right back. Mike will get mad and start a fight. Here is a different approach:

Mike: "Here's your report. You made a few stupid mistakes."

Bill: "Stupid?"

Mike: "Yeah, there are several misspellings."

Bill: "Mike, are you calling me stupid because there are misspellings?"

Mike: "Yeah ... I mean, no ... well, you should have caught them."

Bill: "I probably did make some mistakes, but are you calling me stupid because of it?"

Mike: "No I'm not. I just think that you should have caught it, or used the spell check."

In this example Bill **asks questions** instead of hurling insults. He puts Mike on the defensive without using anger. Bill's questions point out how Mike is out of line. Bill is able to stay calm, and Mike is held accountable for his poor choice of words.

Ask Questions!

One of the most powerful methods of deflecting a verbal baseball is to repeat an offending word in the form of a question. In the previous example, Bill simply said, "Stupid?" which put Mike off balance and forced him to explain his reasons for calling Bill stupid.

Following are some simple but powerful questions that deflect baseballs. Each is useful for different situations. Here are some situations with questions you can use to deflect a baseball.

Situation	What You'd Hear	Deflecting Questions
Someone invades your privacy:	"Are you dating Nancy?"	"Why do you ask?"
Someone is sarcastic:	"Look! It's the genius!"	"What are you saying?"
	"And here comes Mr. Punctual!"	"What do you mean by that?"
Someone uses an insulting word:	"You're so stupid!"	"Stupid?"
	"You're irresponsible!"	"Irresponsible?"
	"What a loser you are!"	"A loser?"
Someone "speaks for everyone else":	"Everyone says you can't stand the boss."	"What do you think?"

Examples of Asking Questions

1. When someone is prying into your privacy:

When someone is nosy, ask this question: *"Why do you ask?"* (Notice how Tommy asks questions to keep Sophia off balance.)

> Sophia: "Hey Tommy, are you and your girlfriend breaking up?"
>
> Tommy: "Why do you ask?"
>
> Sophia: "I don't know, I was just curious. So tell me, are you?"
>
> Tommy: "So you want me to discuss a private matter with you?"
>
> Sophia: "Yeah."
>
> Tommy: "Why would I do that?"

2. The "mouthpiece" who speaks for someone else:

This person acts like he's speaking for other people when he's really hiding his own opinions. The best way to deal with these people is to make them speak for themselves by asking, *"What do you think?"*

> Steve: "Hey Tracy, everyone thinks you're not doing your fair share of the work."
>
> Tracy: "They do? Well tell me Steve, what do you think?"
>
> Steve: "Me? Uh, I don't think that."
>
> Tracy: "Good. Can I count on you to defend me when others say that?"
>
> Steve: "Uh, sure."

3. When someone is sarcastic:

"What are you saying?" or *"What do you mean by that?"* are two great questions to highlight sarcasm.

> Jim: "Hey Tanisha, glad to see you finally made it to work."
>
> Tanisha: "What do you mean by that, Jim?"
>
> Jim: "Um, nothing."

EXERCISE: Deflecting Baseballs

Directions: With a partner take turns reading the following statements aloud. One partner reads a statement, and the other responds with an approrpiate deflecting question.

Example: "That's a stupid idea."
Deflection: "Stupid?"

1. "Hey, is it true you're dating Terry?"

_____

2. "Why do you wear those ridiculous clothes all the time?"

_____

3. "Well look here, it's the boss's best friend."

_____

4. "You there, Mr./Ms. know-it-all, I have a question."

_____

5. "Hey, I saw you talking to the boss. What were you talking about?"

_____

6. "Everyone says you are difficult to work with these days."

_____

7. "I'd ask you to help, but I need someone dependable."

_____

8. (Sarcastically) "Excuse me genius, may I ask you a question?"

_____

HOMEWORK: Deflecting Baseballs

PART 1

Directions: Circle the best answer for deflecting these baseball statements.

1. "That was an idiotic thing to do!"

A. "I'm not an idiot, you are!"   C. "Who are you calling an idiot?"
B. "Idiotic?"   D. "I know. I'll try harder."

2. "Why are you wearing those weird clothes?"

A. "Because I like them."   C. "Why do you ask?"
B. "What's wrong with them?"   D. "Mind your own business."

3. "So people think you stole the money missing from the cash register."

A. "Who? Who said that?"   C. "They do? I'm not a thief! I wasn't
B. "What do you think?"   even there that night!"
                             D. "Are you calling me a thief?"

4. "The boss doesn't favor me as she does you."

A. "What do you mean by that?" C. "Why would she? I'm better than you."
B. "Favor me?"   D. "So, how was your weekend?"

PART 2

Directions: On the lines below, fill in your response to these baseballs.

1. "So, are you having marital problems?"

_____

2. "Everyone says you got the job because you're friends with the boss."

_____

3. "How can you eat such strange food?"

_____

Dealing with Serious Insults: Deflecting Bullets

A **bullet** is a very serious insult, one that is extremely cruel and hurtful. Address such insults directly and assertively. However, as with a "baseball insult" don't respond with rage or violence, but with controlled, assertive behavior. The best method is the steps you learned in the chapter, Starting Difficult Conversations. Once again, those steps are:

1. **State the facts.**

2. **State how you feel.**

3. **State your need.**

Poor Example:

Ann: "Devon, the printer is broken. It's stupid idiots like you who keep breaking it."

Devon: "Stupid idiots? I think you are the stupid idiot!"

In this example, Devon responded to the insult (bullet) with anger and his own insult. From that point the conversation would spiral into an exchange of harsher insults, or worse. Here is a better approach:

Better Example:

Ann: "Devon, the printer is broken. It's stupid idiots like you who keep breaking it."

Devon: "Hey Ann, I'm willing to talk about the printer, but when you call me a stupid idiot *(fact)* I feel insulted *(feeling)* and I need you to take back that comment *(need)* if we are going to have this conversation."

In this example Devon used facts, feelings, and needs to say, "I'm willing to work with you on this issue, but the insults must stop."

Hand Out/Hand Up

Picture yourself putting one hand out, "I'm willing to talk," and the other hand up, "but the insults have to stop." In the first example below, Christina responds with anger.

Nick: "You're late with the report again. I can't believe you. I don't know why the boss tolerates such a loser around here."

Christina: "Loser? You're the loser. I wouldn't have been late with the report if you'd given me the right information to start with."

Now here's an example of Christina responding with the "hand out, hand up" method.

"I'm willing to talk with you..."
(hand out)

Nick: "You're late with the report again. I can't believe you. I don't know why the boss tolerates such a loser around here."

Christina: "Look Nick, I'm willing to discuss the fact that the report is late *(hand out)*, but I feel insulted when you call me a loser, and I need you not to call me that so we can solve this problem, okay?" *(hand up)*

Quite often people in conflict are frustrated, angry, nervous, or scared. Leading with the hand out ("I'm willing to keep talking...") lets someone know you're still open, before you put your hand up and tell him what you think he did wrong ("but I felt insulted... and I need you to stop...").

"... but the insults need to stop."
(Hand up) is a great way to deal with someone sending verbal bullets at you.

If someone is violent or enraged or irrational, none of these tools will work. It may make sense simply to walk away. Some may say that walking away is a sign of weakness. But by walking away when someone is irrational or potentially violent, you stay calm and safe and you look like the reasonable, rational person.

EXERCISE: Managing Bullets

Directions: Each of the following exercises is the beginning of a conversation that involves conflict. Each ends with one of the participants shooting verbal bullets at the other.

Reader 2 must respond to the bullets by using the facts, feelings, needs, and hand out/hand up. Notice that Reader 2 uses the active listening tools (simple signals, mirroring, paraphrasing) to handle angry Reader 1.

EXERCISE ❶ Two co-workers have been working on a report together.

Reader 1: "I've had it with you!"

Reader 2: "You're upset." *(mirroring)* "What's wrong?" *(tell me more)*

Reader 1: "We just got the report back from the boss. She rejected it because your graphs are incomplete. We have one day to fix it and hand it back."

Reader 2: "So you're upset with me because you think I didn't do my part?" *(paraphrases)*

Reader 1: "Yes! I can't believe I have to work with an idiot like you!"

Reader 2: Respond to the "idiot" bullet.

_____

_____

EXERCISE ❷ Two co-workers are talking about a project at work.

Reader 1: "What is it with you?"

Reader 2: "Wow, you seem upset." *(mirroring)* "What's wrong?" *(tell me more)*

Reader 1: "I just found out you lent our color printer to Accounting for the next two weeks. What is with that? How am I going to finish my project?"

Reader 2: "So you're upset because you need the printer and I lent it out?" *(paraphrasing)*

Reader 1: "Yes!"

Reader 2: "Okay, can I tell you why I did that?" *(asks to push the talk button)*

Reader 1: "All right, but make it quick."

Reader 2: "Accounting borrowed the printer, but they promised to return it and help you meet the deadline on your project."

Reader 1: "What? Those guys in Accounting can't help me! They're just as useless as you are!"

Reader 2: Respond to the "useless" bullet.

_____

_____

EXERCISE ❸ **A husband and wife are talking about scheduling problems.**

Husband: "Dear, what time do you want to go over to my parents' tonight?"

Wife: "What? We're going to your parents'?"

Husband: "Yes, we talked about it last week."

Wife: "What? No way! Not again!"

Husband: "You sound frustrated." *(mirroring)*

Wife: "I am! Besides, we're always going over there! And I have too much work to do."

Husband: "So you're very busy, and you're tired of going over to my folks' house." *(paraphrasing)*

Wife: "Yes. Besides, I can't stand them. And your mom is a terrible cook. She's the reason you can't even boil water."

Husband: Respond to the " boil water" bullet.

_____

_____

EXERCISE ❹ **Two housemates are having problems with unpaid bills.**

Reader 1: "We need to talk NOW!"

Reader 2: "What's wrong?" *(tell me more)* "You're really upset." *(mirroring)*

Reader 1: "Upset? Of course I'm upset! The phone company just cut off our line because once AGAIN you didn't pay our bill. My name is on the bill! Now my credit is ruined!"

Reader 2: "I can see why you'd be upset." *(acknowledges)* "I'm sorry about this."

Reader 1: "Sorry? You're sorry all right! You are the sorriest person I've ever shared a house with! I can't believe I let a deadbeat like you take charge of paying bills!"

Reader 2: Respond to the "deadbeat" bullet.

_____

_____

HOMEWORK: Hand Out/Hand Up Exercise

PART 1

Directions: Think of a verbal bullet that someone has shot at you. Briefly describe it below.

1. Describe the bullet: _____

_____

PART 2

Directions: Now use the situation above to practice a controlled assertive response using the hand out/hand up exercise.

Hand out: "Hey, _____, I'm willing to _____.

Hand up: "But I felt _____ when you

_____ and I need you to _____

so we can continue to discuss this."

PART 3

Directions: Deflect the bullet below. Write exactly what you would say using the "hand out, hand up" method.

Friend: *(angry)* "What is with you?"
You: "What's wrong?" *(simple signal)*
Friend: "Wrong? You borrowed my car last night and left the lights on! I came out this morning and found a dead battery! I was half-an-hour late for work! The boss is on my case now!"
You: "So you're upset because my mistake made you late for work." *(paraphrase)*
Friend: "Yes, you idiot! Of course I'm upset! Did you think I'd be happy?"

Deflect the bullet: _____

_____

Managing Conflict

Conflict is unavoidable. We all have disagreements with family members, co-workers, friends, and bosses. Since everyone experiences conflict, it is wise to be prepared for it, just as you would be prepared for an emergency such as a fire or flood. This section provides some ideas for managing conflict situations. They include:

- Keeping yourself calm

- Calming others

- Thinking "win-win"

You will find that managing conflict includes using common sense, and the communication skills you have already learned in this book.

"Only two things in life are certain—death and taxes."

—Benjamin Franklin

**"Actually, three things in life are certain—
death, taxes, and conflict with others.
Unfortunately, conflict is the only one
you can talk your way out of."**

—Dan Farley and Cindy Donaldson

Keeping Yourself Calm

Conflict is almost always a negative experience that we relate to shouting, hurt feelings, damaged relationships, even violence. For that reason, we become very tense in conflict situations. When you are tense or afraid you might have trouble thinking and speaking clearly. After a conflict, have you ever said to yourself, "I wish I'd said this…" or, "Why didn't I think of that?" Tension prevented you from thinking on your feet.

When we are in conflict situations we often "lose it" and let our emotions take over. Usually we regret what we said or did as a result. These comments might sound familiar:

"I was so upset I was speechless!"

"I was so mad I couldn't think."

"I just reacted and started screaming."

A strong physical response dating back to our cave-dwelling ancestors explains why we often seem unable to speak or think clearly in conflict. When faced by a charging tiger, our early ancestors had two choices—fight the tiger or run from it. Over time these survival instincts created a physical reaction we still have today. When we are scared, more of our blood rushes to our limbs—our arms (to fight) and our legs (to flee). With less blood in the brain, we're not able to think as clearly. So the challenge in conflict situations is to remain calm, which keeps the blood in our brains so we can think clearly.

Here are two simple ways to stay calm when conflict arises.

Take Time to Calm Down

It is difficult to think clearly when you are upset. We often react immediately to conflict, and later regret our actions in that emotional moment.

Our fight or flee reactions to conflict date back to our ancestors and how they dealt with such threats.

To stay calm in a conflict situation, **take time to compose yourself**. There is no right amount of time; each situation is different. Confronting someone in private is almost always better than doing so in public, and waiting for an opportunity to talk privately with him or her provides time to calm down. But waiting too long to react can be just as inappropriate as reacting too quickly; people can forget situations if you react much later.

EXERCISE: Reaction Time

Directions: Below are brief descriptions of potential conflict situations. Each is followed by some suggested reaction times. For each situation select the most appropriate time to wait before reacting. List the reasons for your choice.

Example: A talkative co-worker interrupts you three times in a meeting.

A. Address it immediately in the meeting.
B. Talk to him about it when you go to lunch next week.
C. Talk to him about it right after the meeting.

Your choice: C Reasons: Gives me a few minutes to calm down, yet addresses it soon enough that he will remember it. He's not annoying me intentionally, and talking to him privately is probably more appropriate.

1. You and a co-worker were responsible for a presentation to senior managers. Your co-worker missed the meeting, and you made the presentation yourself. You did the best you could, but looked unprepared and disorganized without your co-worker's material. The meeting is over and you need to talk to your co-worker.

A. Wait a week.
B. Discuss it the next time you are scheduled to give a presentation.
C. Wait 30-60 minutes.
D. Go find her now.

Your choice _____

Reasons_____

_____

2. A co-worker makes an insulting joke about your clothes in front of everyone at a staff meeting.

A. Deal with it right there.
B. Talk to him immediately after the meeting.
C. Wait an hour.
D. Wait a week.

Your choice _____

Reasons_____

3. You carpool with a co-worker. She's speeding, changing lanes suddenly, and cutting off other drivers. You don't feel safe.

A. React right away.
B. Take two minutes to compose yourself.
C. Talk to her about it when you get to work.
D. Take ten seconds to compose yourself.

Your choice _____

Reasons_____

Know Your "Hot Buttons"

Another way to stay calm and avoid losing control is to be aware of words and actions that set you off and cause you to shut down or lose control. These are our **"hot buttons."**

"Hot buttons" are things that people **do or say** that cause us to get extremely upset. Each of us has our own list of hot buttons. Here are some examples:

Did something	Said something
Laughed at you	Called you a name
Interrupted you	Ridiculed you
Ignored you	Made a joke about you

Like conflict, it is inevitable that people will push your hot buttons, and they usually aren't aware that they are doing it. Since you cannot avoid it entirely, the best way to prepare is to be aware of what sets you off and might cause you to lose control. In the next exercise, identify your hot buttons and your typical reactions. Identifying and discussing them will help you prepare for the next time someone pushes one of your hot buttons. Being more aware of what sets you off may possibly diminish the strong feelings you have when it happens.

EXERCISE: "Knowing Your Hot Buttons"

Directions: Think of some things that people say or do that push your hot buttons. Then write how you react when you "lose it." Share with a partner what pushes your hot buttons and how you react.

Hot Button	Reaction

Example:
Someone interrupts me   *Get angry, then yell.*

1. _____   _____

   _____   _____

2. _____   _____

   _____   _____

3. _____   _____

   _____   _____

Calming Down Others

The only person you can control is yourself, but there are some things you can do when you are in conflict with others to help them calm down. First, be aware that they, too, have hot buttons and you or someone else might have pushed one or more of those buttons. Second, use the active listening skills you have learned in this book to help others feel understood.

Watch for signs

Knowing your own hot buttons helps *you* stay calm when they are pushed. Knowing when you have pushed someone else's hot buttons helps you know when you must calm *them* down. We all know how to push the hot buttons of our friends, co-workers, or family members. And we know how they act when they're upset. Obvious signs are yelling and physical aggression. For the categories below, describe in more detail what these signs would look like.

Signs of Tension

Body posture _____

Eye contact _____

Face _____

Voice _____

Words _____

Use Active Listening to Calm Others

While we may know some of the ways we push people's hot buttons, we rarely intend to do it. Most often we say or do something unintentionally that suddenly upsets another.

The reasons someone is angry may have nothing to do with us. For example, a restaurant manager might be faced with a customer who is furious about a waiter's rude service. The manager did not directly cause the problem, but he still needs to calm the customer.

Whether or not you caused the problem, the best approach is active listening. Think of the conflict onion once again. When people are upset, they have strong feelings. Peeling away the feelings about the facts usually leads to resolution.

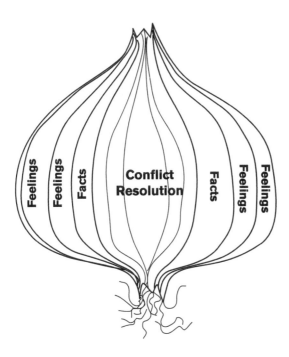

You have seen this onion before, so you know that to get to resolution, peel away feelings and facts with active listening.

Following is an example of how someone can unexpectedly push another person's hot button, then use active listening to calm her down quickly.

Brian and Leslie are co-workers. They just completed a lengthy project, and they are meeting to discuss how it went. Without intending to, Brian immediately pushes one of Leslie's hot buttons.

Brian: "Okay, we finally finished the project! Let's go over it and see what we could have done better."

Leslie: (Suddenly looking upset, her face flushed) "Oh great, that's just what I want to do," she says sarcastically.

Brian: "Wow, you look upset. *(mirrors)* What's wrong?" *(tell me more)*

Leslie: "I am. We worked like dogs on this project for months, and got a big contract out of it. I'd like to review some of the positive things first before we criticize ourselves."

Brian: "So you want to acknowledge our success first, then look at what we could improve." *(paraphrases)*

Leslie: "Yeah."

Brian: "Okay. I can see why you would feel that way. So let's go over our accomplishments first."

Brian recognized quickly that he had unintentionally pressed one of Leslie's hot buttons. First, he calmed her down by mirroring to reflect her feelings, then got to the facts with a "tell me more" statement. Finally he showed that he understood the facts by paraphrasing.

Conflict can come up quickly, and as Brian experienced, you don't always see it coming. His skillful resolution of the problem is an example of a phrase to remember:

"When you find yourself in trouble, active listen on the double."

Since you have learned active listening skills already, and have had opportunities to practice them throughout this book, *you don't have to learn anything new to handle conflict*. If you use these active listening tools effectively, you will be calm and in control when conflict arises!

A summary review of the communication skills we have covered will remind you of the tools you have available to manage conflict.

Your Communication Toolkit

Would you use a hammer to saw a board? Of course not! By reading this book you have learned some useful communication tools. However, each communication tool, just like a hand tool, is best suited for specific situations.

The chart on the next page lists the communication tools that are most effective for specific conflict situations.

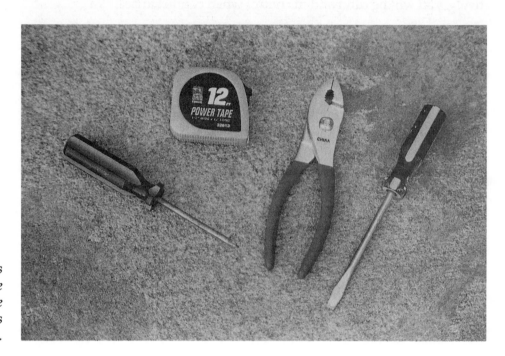

Each of these tools has a specific use. The same is true for the communication skills you now know.

Your Communication Toolkit

Situation	Example	Tool	Example
You hear only feelings.	"I've had it with you!"	Mirror.	"You look upset."
		Tell me more.	"Tell me what's wrong."
You get just facts.	"I think a pay raise would cheer up everyone ."	Paraphrase.	"So you think higher salaries would increase morale."
You get feelings and facts.	"I'm angry that you've lied to me again!"	Paraphrase.	"So you're upset because I keep misleading you."
The other person refuses to cooperate.	"Oh stop being so sensitive!"	Paraphrase their "facts only" reply.	"So you think I'm being too sensitive by asking you to stop calling me that name?"
You are mildly insulted (baseball).	"Why are you wearing that stupid hat?"	Ask questions.	"Stupid?"
You are very insulted (bullet).	"You are such a loser!"	Hand out.	"I'm willing to talk about this."
		Hand up: facts, feelings, needs.	"But I feel insulted when you call me a loser, and I need you to stop saying that."
You want to explain your point to an upset person.		Calm them down with active listening.	Simple signals, mirroring, Paraphrasing.
		Use understanding statements.	"I see your point now."
		Ask to push the talk button.	"May I tell you my views?"

Think "Win-Win"

Finally, the third way to manage conflict is to approach it with the best possible intentions. When we are in conflict we think, "How can I win this argument?" The answer is, you can't. If you make a point of defeating people in conflicts by putting them down, shouting, or intimidating, you hurt those relationships. This is "win-lose" conflict: you win and the other person loses, and may very well seek revenge later. Your opponent's revenge may lead you to attack again, and an endless cycle of conflict continues.

In the workplace people are dependent on each other in order to get the job done. Approaching conflict with a "win-lose" attitude will damage your relationships, hinder your ability to get your job done, and hurt the organization.

The best way to approach conflict is "win-win." This approach involves seeking solutions that work for everyone. Here are some questions that promote a win-win outcome.

How can we each get what we need in this situation?

Are there ways we can satisfy both of our needs?

How can we resolve this together?

Notice that these questions are a form of active listening. By asking them, you show that you are open to hearing what the other person wants, which invites cooperation. While these questions may lead to your compromising on some of your points, it will start to calm the other person, and increase the chance of an agreeable solution.

EXERCISE: Conflict Management

Directions: Following are four conflict situations. Read the speaker's lines, then write your response on the lines provided. If you answer correctly, the next line down should sound like a proper response.

SITUATION ❶

A co-worker says to you, "That's it! I can't take you anymore!"

Your response: _____

"You're darned right I'm upset! You took the Thursday shift again. That's the third time this month! Now I have to work on the weekend!"

Your response: _____

"Yes! I'm tired of getting last picks! You work the weekend for once!"

Your response: _____

"All right, but make it snappy."

Your response: _____

"I don't care about that! I have things I need to do this weekend, too! Just because you kiss up to the boss like some wimp shouldn't mean I have to work every weekend!"

Your response: _____

SITUATION ❷

A friend of yours rushes up to you looking very angry and says, "What's with you?"

Your response: _____

"What's wrong? I'll tell you what's wrong! For three weeks I've been waiting for you to pay me back! You said you'd pay me in two days, and I still haven't seen one cent of the $50 I lent you. That's what's wrong!"

Your response: _____

Yes, that's why I'm upset. So when am I going to see my money?"

SITUATION ❸

You are extremely late getting home for dinner. Someone is waiting for you, very angry, and says, "Where have you been?"

Your response: _____

"Of course I'm upset. You promised you'd be home two hours ago! I've been waiting, not knowing when you'd be here. Dinner is cold. Go serve yourself."

Your response: _____

"Yes, you specifically promised you'd be home on time! This is the third time in two weeks I've been left waiting for you."

Your response: _____

Yes, it's not like the first time it's happened! I'm sick of these broken promises."

Your response: _____

That's right. Look, I know you're busy. But I need to know when you're going to be home."

SITUATION ④

Your housemate is very annoyed with you and says, "Who do you think I am, your personal maid?"

Your response: _____

Of course I'm upset! You would be too if someone left a kitchen full of dirty dishes for you to clean up!"

Your response: _____

"Yes, we agreed I'd do the cooking, and you'd do the dishes! I'm making you great meals, but you haven't washed a single dish!"

Your response: _____

"Yes, I held up my end of the bargain. You should do your part. You eat like a pig, and you clean up like one too."

Your response: _____

HOMEWORK: Identify the Communication Tool

Directions: Below are some conflict situations. In each situation, Speaker 2 uses active listening to calm Speaker 1. On the lines provided, write the communication skill that Speaker 2 uses, such as simple signals and mirroring. Review page 195 for other listening tools.

SITUATION ❶

Speaker 1: "You've done it this time!

Speaker 2: "Wow, you're upset. What's wrong?"

Communication tool(s): _____

Speaker 1: "What's wrong? I'll tell you what's wrong! I had a full tank of gas yesterday before you drove my car, and now I'm on empty!"

Speaker 2: "So you're upset because you think I used all the gas?"

Communication tool(s): _____

SITUATION ❷

Speaker 1: "You! You idiot! I want to talk to you!"

Speaker 2: "Idiot?"

Communication tool(s): _____

Speaker 1: "Yeah, you're an idiot. You forgot to tell me about the meeting yesterday. I looked bad not being there.

Speaker 2: "So you think I was responsible for reminding you about the meeting?

Communication tool(s): _____

Speaker 1: "Yeah."

Speaker 2: "What led you to believe that?"

Communication tool(s): _____

Name:_____

SITUATION 3

Speaker 1: "I've had it with you."
Speaker 2: "What's wrong? You sound upset."

Communication tool(s): _____

Speaker 1: "I just can't believe you."
Speaker 2: "Well, tell me more."

Communication tool(s): _____

Speaker 1: "You totally forgot we were going to the movies tonight. I've been
           waiting for an hour. Now it's too late."
Speaker 2: "So you're mad because I let you down."

Communication tool(s): _____

Speaker 1: "You're darned right I am! I can't count on you anymore!"
Speaker 2: " So you're tired of my not meeting my commitments?"

Communication Tool(s): _____

Getting Agreements

Remember, at the center of the onion is "Conflict Resolution." At this point both sides have listened to each other, and have come to some agreement that will satisfy them.

Some conflicts are difficult for various reasons: the issues are complex, or one side is difficult and will not cooperate. This section does not deal with complex conflict situations. These skills are called negotiation skills, and many good books are available on that topic. Fortunately most everyday conflict situations are uncomplicated emotional issues that can be solved with the communication skills you now have. This section shows you how to **get agreements** in conflict situations with a few simple steps.

1. **Draw out and understand the other person.**

2. **State your needs.**

3. **Summarize your agreements.**

A common mistake in resolving conflict is not making sure both sides agree on a solution. Later this oversight can lead to misunderstandings and even more conflict. If you don't have a clear agreement, people might feel misled or tricked later on. This section shows you how to avoid such misunderstandings.

Using good communication skills is the key to getting agreements that work for you and others.

Draw Out and Understand the Other

You have reached the center of the onion by peeling away feelings, then getting the facts. You've peeled away those layers with active listening. So when you get to the center of the onion you have a pretty good idea of people's needs. Confirm your understanding of their needs with a paraphrase:

"So let me make sure I understand here, Joe. You want me to pay you back the twenty dollars, plus an extra five bucks for forgetting?"

"Let me make sure I've gotten what you need, Jody. You want me to work your weekend shift and you'll cover my late night shift?"

Remember, *paraphrasing is a question*. If you misunderstand, they'll let you know. In addition, paraphrasing doesn't mean you are agreeing; you are only trying to understand their viewpoint.

If you have difficulty understanding, even after paraphrasing, then ask what they need. Here are some phrases to use:

"So what do you need from me?" (Ask positively, not sarcastically, of course.)

"What can I do to solve the problem?"

EXERCISE: Asking What They Need

Directions: Write down other questions that would draw out someone's needs.

Example:
What will solve the problem for you?

1. _____

2. _____

3. _____

State Your Needs

Before you state your needs, be sure you understand the other person. Not only do you avoid confusion, but you help to calm him because he feels heard.

People are more willing to compromise and negotiate if they just feel heard. So use your active listening to make life easier! Then you can present your point of view, which is a skill you've already learned.

If someone disagrees completely, go back to active listening and attempt to draw out ideas that will satisfy both of you. Remember, if you get disagreement, presenting your side louder is not the solution!

The steps from Pressing the Talk Button, remind you how to state your needs.

1. **Actively listen.** (Let's assume you've already done that.)
2. **Make an understanding statement.**
3. **Ask to state your needs.** (Make sure the other person is ready to listen.)
4. **State your needs.**

These steps are presented in detail in the section, Pressing the Talk Button, so here is a summary example.

Oscar: "I understand what you're looking for now."
    (understanding statement)
    "May I tell you what I need here?"
    (asks to press the talk button)

Lynn: "Okay."

Oscar: "I'll pick you up on time if you promise to be ready
    when I arrive. Okay? How does that sound?" *(presents
    his needs)*

Small phrases like, "How does that sound?" show that you are receptive to the other person's request.

EXERCISE: Inviting Phrases

Directions: Think of a few phrases you could use after stating your needs to invite the other person's response:

Example:
"How does that sound?"

1. _____

2. _____

3. _____

Summarize

Finally, when you reach agreement, summarize your understanding. Summarizing is just another paraphrase, but it is important because it avoids confusion and frustration later!

> "So we agree that you'll take care of printing and copying the report, and I'll handle distribution?"

> "Let's summarize what we've agreed upon: I wash the car, and you take care of maintenance?"

> "So let me clarify what we've agreed to. You'll provide new product training to the sales force, and I'll train the service technicians?" Does that sound right to you?

Remember, if there's confusion when you summarize, go right back to active listening to clear up misunderstandings!

HOMEWORK: Practice Summarizing

Directions: Name two situations in which you had disagreements with someone and worked out a solution. On the lines provided, briefly describe the situations, and summarize your agreements. Write the summary as if you were speaking to the other person.

Example:

I share a computer with a co-worker. She likes to "surf the Web" at lunch, but that is time I often use to catch up on work. We agreed that she can surf the Web, but if I have work to do she'll let me use the computer.

Summarizing Statement:

"Okay, let me see if I understand our agreement. We agree that you can surf the Web at lunch, but if I need the computer for work you'll let me use it. And I'll do my best to minimize the times that I need to do work at lunch."

1. My Situation

_____

_____

Summarizing Statement:

"Okay, let me see if I understand our agreement. _____

_____

_____

2. My Situation

_____

_____

Summarizing Statement:

"Okay, let me see if I understand our agreement. _____

_____

_____

Communicating Effectively in a Diverse Workplace

In today's workplace your co-workers come from many different backgrounds, including nationality, gender, and age. The ability to work with others in a diverse workplace and to understand and to respect differences is a skill valued by employers. This section examines some ways to do that.

Diversity Is Not Just Ethnic

When workforce diversity is discussed, you probably think of ethnic or racial diversity. But there are many other factors that make up a diverse workforce. Just a few of these factors are:

- Age
- Gender
- Where someone was raised
- How someone was raised
- Even personality style!

And there are many more factors that affect the way people behave, and how they interact with others. Consider this typical workplace team.

- Minh is 22, of Vietnamese dissent, born in Colorado.
- Mary is 42, African-American, born in New York.
- JoAnne is 25, Caucasian, born in Germany.
- Mark is 61, Caucasian, born in Florida.
- Anthony is 23, of Guatemalan dissent, born in California.
- Huy is 35, born in Vietnam.

If you were a member of this team, you would be wise to consider more than just ethnicity when interacting with your teammates. For example, Minh and Huy have the same Vietnamese ethnicity, but were raised in different countries. Considering only ethnicity would overlook other parts of your teammates' backgrounds that also determine how you can interact with them most effectively.

EXERCISE: What Else Defines Diversity?

Directions: Form small groups and list other characteristics or backgrounds of people that also contribute to diversity.

1. _____

2 _____

3. _____

Be Aware of Customs...

Customs are commonly accepted behaviors for a particular group and are often associated with ethnicity. But customs are not based on just ethnicity; any group can have customs. Customs are based on nationality, age, family, or regional origin (where you grew up), to name a few. Here are some comments you might hear, all of which describe customs.

"In my family, elders are respected."

"In my country, honor of family is most important."

"My generation values reputation more than wealth."

Notice that three different customs are described based on three different social groups: family, country, and generation. **Because customs of social groups vary widely, it is impossible to know them all.**

For example, Jeff, a co-worker, was raised in a military family and served in the military himself. A custom for him, based upon how he was raised and his occupational background, is to refer to a manager as "sir" or "ma'am." If you did not know about this custom, you might think Jeff was overly formal or perhaps sarcastic. Being aware of customs important to co-workers helps you gain insight into how they prefer to interact.

... Beware of Generalizations

While customs are helpful for understanding *some* of the behaviors of others, they can be misleading. Generalizing about someone because of appearance or background is risky, as the following example shows.

Ed and Frank are co-workers. Ed is Asian, Frank is not. They are discussing a plan to talk to the boss about a proposal she recently presented.

> Frank: "Someone needs to tell the boss about the problems with her proposal. I'm assuming you wouldn't want to do it."
>
> Ed: "Why do you say that?"
>
> Frank: "Well, in Asian culture isn't it considered extremely disrespectful to disagree with a superior?"
>
> Ed: "That may be true, but I was born and raised in Arizona."
>
> Frank: "Oh."
>
> Ed: "And besides, there is no one Asian culture. There are lots of countries in Asia. Making assumptions about me based on my Asian race is sort of like generalizing about someone as North American when they were born in Chicago."
>
> Frank: "Oh."
>
> Ed: "And I would be glad to talk with the boss about the proposal. Since I have worked on a project similar to what she is proposing, I think I would be pretty convincing with regard to the problems we see."

In this example Frank used a cultural generalization to make assumptions about Ed's approach to the problem of talking with the boss. As Frank became painfully aware, both the generalization and the assumption did not fit.

Your Communication Skills Help to Manage Diversity

So how do you communicate effectively in a diverse workplace, when you cannot rely on generalizations? The answer is to treat each person individually and watch, listen, and ask how they prefer to interact. These are skills you have already learned in this book.

Watch and Listen

In the earlier sections on personality styles you learned to determine the styles of others by watching how they move and by listening to what they say. This same approach helps you to determine how to interact with others in a diverse environment.

Our own behaviors reflect how we like for others to interact with us. Someone who is talkative and energetic usually responds well to others with a similar approach. So rather than assume you know how to interact with someone because she is Australian, or over fifty, for instance, watch and listen to how she interacts with others. Your observations will give you clues about her communication style and preferences.

Don't Assume, Ask

To work effectively in a diverse workplace it is a good idea to inquire about behaviors you are unsure of. Assuming you know why someone behaves in a certain way is risky. The technique of, "facts, check it out," from the section, Playing Jazz in Difficult Conversations, is effective for discovering the reasons behind someone's behavior. Here is an example of how "facts, check it out," is useful.

Jenny and Ming are co-workers at the High Tech Software Company. Everyone at the company has been working hard for months on a big project. The company put on a party at work one afternoon to help employees relieve some stress and celebrate their success. There was food, music, and some "stress busting" activities. One of them involved employees throwing balls at a target next to a water tank. Above the tank, managers of the company sat on a platform. If the employees hit the target, the managers would fall into the water. Everyone took a turn throwing at the target except Ming, who left the party and went back to work.

When Jenny saw Ming later, she asked him about what happened.

> Jenny: "Ming, you left the party early. Is everything okay?"
> *(facts, check it out)*

> Ming: "Well actually, that kind of activity makes me uncomfortable. Where I grew up, people would never disrespect managers like that. So I didn't want to participate."

> Jenny: "Oh, I had no idea you felt that way. I'm sorry it was uncomfortable for you."

Jenny used the "facts, check it out" technique to find the reasons for Ming's behavior. She didn't make an assumption that he was anti-social, or accuse him of not being a team player because he left the party early. Jenny learned something about Ming's background that will be helpful for her in future interactions with him. This is another way you can use the communication tools you have learned to work effectively in a diverse workplace.

Build Working Relationships

To work effectively in a diverse workplace, take the time to build working relationships with co-workers. Your communication skills, like active listening and providing positive feedback, are effective ways to build familiarity and trust with co-workers, which will help you understand how best to interact with them. Following are some simple yet effective ways to build relationships in the workplace.

- Take the time to thank a co-worker for something he has done for you.

- Periodically chat with others during a coffee break instead of reading the newspaper.

- Consult a co-worker on an area of expertise she might have.

- Take an interest in pictures or awards someone displays in her office.

This is not to suggest that you become a social butterfly at work or pry into people's lives. Respecting privacy is also essential to good working relationships. Not all of the suggestions above involve socializing; some simply use opportunities in everyday work to interact more with co-workers. Familiarity and basic interaction with the people who work next to you every day start to build trust in the workplace. When people share a basic level of trust, they are more likely to respect differences in a diverse workplace.

EXERCISE: Acknowledging Similarities and Differences

Directions: Below are topics or situations in which people might have different behaviors. Break into small groups and discuss group members' preferences for each. If possible, identify where you think your own preferences come from. There is no right answer! The point is to note where preferences are alike and to recognize and respect differences.

Example:

Eye contact

Bill: "I was always taught to look people straight in the eye. So I do that, and I like it when others do the same."

Joan: "I grew up in Japan and was taught that it was disrespectful to look elders in the eye."

Martin: "I don't really pay attention to eye contact. Although I hate it when people try to intimidate me with too much direct eye contact."

1. Standing close (during conversation, on an elevator, etc.)

2. Greeting, i.e. shaking hands

3. Touching (hand on shoulder, hug, pat on the back)

4. Interrupting when speaking

5. Treatment of superiors (like a boss)

6. Body language messages

7. Small talk

8. Table manners

9. Phone etiquette

10. Disagreeing with the opinions of others (i.e., public vs. private)

EXERCISE: Building Work Relationships

Directions: List five other ways you can build relationships with co-workers. Include a mix of social opportunities, like company parties, and non-social opportunities, like thanking a co-worker for something.

1. _____

2. _____

3. _____

4. _____

5. _____

Impressing Employers with Your Communication Skills

As mentioned in the introduction, managers spend a lot of their time dealing with communication issues among employees. Therefore, managers put a great deal of emphasis on communication skills when hiring. If you have learned the communication techniques in this book, you have a very marketable skill that will impress prospective employers. This section helps you prepare to answer questions about your communication skills that might come up in a job interview. Spend some time planning your answers to these questions, and you will stand out from the competition in the job market!

Types of Interview Questions

Employers typically ask two types of questions in a job interview: **open-ended questions** and **situational questions.**

Open-ended questions cannot be answered with a simple yes or no. They are designed to get you talking, to see how much you know about a particular topic.

Situational questions describe a scenario and ask how you would address it. They are designed to see how you would handle certain situations in the workplace.

What follows are some open-ended and situational questions you might be asked in an interview about the major topics in this text. Practice answering them and you'll find yourself prepared and confident, which impresses employers.

Personality Styles and Stretching

1. There are many different people in the workplace. How do you handle people who have a style different from your own?

_____

_____

_____

2. One of our key customers, I'll call him Bill, is a really demanding guy. He's short on words, and wants action quickly. How would you handle someone like this?

_____

_____

_____

Starting Difficult Conversations

1. What do you do when you have a conflict with another co-worker?

_____

_____

_____

2. You think that one of your co-workers isn't doing his fair share of a project you are working on together. How would you address this problem with him?

_____

_____

_____

Listening Skills

1. Things are pretty fast-paced here. We can't afford to have miscommunications. Tell me about your listening skills.

_____

_____

_____

2. What would you do if I gave you a complicated assignment and you weren't quite sure you understood it.

_____

_____

_____

Conflict Management

1. How do you handle difficult people?

_____

_____

_____

2. You have a co-worker who keeps handing you incomplete work. You talk to her about it and she just laughs at you and says, "If you don't like it, fix it yourself." How would you handle her?

_____

_____

_____

Notes

Notes

Notes

Notes

Notes

Notes